THE TWO VERSIONS OF

King Lear

ORSOLYA LAURA PÉTERFY

Paperback: 978-1-959224-29-7
eBook: 978-1-959224-30-3
Library of Congress Control Number: 2022921969

Graphic Design by Hunor László Péterfy

Ordering Information:

Prime Seven Media
518 Landmann St.
Tomah City, WI 54660

Printed in the United States of America

Table of Contents

Introduction

It is staggering how many misconceptions are circulating about Shakespeare's *King Lear.* While it is clear to me that the useful, readable, and culturally digestible Folio version may be a reworking, it is still more authentic than the faulty Quarto, you should not take it as evidence when one does deeper research. I will look for answers to research questions such as since when may the Folio text be used, why this text is better, and what examples we can list that also set the quarto as a valuable work?

The two versions are: the 1608 quarto printed by Nicholas Oakes for Nathaniel Butter (Q Lear) and the text included in the first folio of Shakespeare (F Lear). "The posthumous publication of the 1623 folio, of course, constituted a major event both in the formation of Shakespeare's authorial canon and in the history of early modern English printed drama. The 1608 text of Lear, on the other hand, as many readers may also know, was disparaged for much of the twentieth century as a "bad" quarto: that is, an ineptly printed, perhaps pirated or memorially reconstructed text, which - in the opinion of a number of prominent Shakespearean textual scholars - represented a gross distortion of the play Shakespeare must have originally written."[1]

Douglas A. Brooks argues as follows: "What may be less well known is that the 1608 text of the play is the only extant printed quarto to prominently feature Shakespeare's name at the top of the title page. At the very least, the rather stark disparity between the singular authorial status of the 1608 Lear quarto and its subsequent inauthorial status in twentieth-century textual scholarship deser ves attention. Indeed, I believe that a careful examination of the specific cultural, material, and

1 Douglas A. Brooks, *"King Lear" (1608) and the Typography of Literary Ambition Author(s).* Source: Renaissance Drama, 1999-2001, New Series, Vol. 30, Institutions of the Text (1999-2001), p. 133.

historical circumstances in which Q Lear was produced sheds much needed light not only on the physical coming into being of one of Shakespeare's most important works but also more generally on the production, circulation, and reception of printed drama."[2] The Folio, on the other hand, created after Shakespeare's death, was published by his fellows.

As a result, the Folio is often considered more authoritative. However, there is a great deal of uncertainty about the relationship between the printed texts and what took place on stage during Shakespeare's lifetime. Some would argue that the differences between the Quarto and the Folio reflect changes made to the play as it was performed in Shakespeare's theatre - changes in which the playwright may or may not have had a hand.

The topic of the dissertation

First of all I intend to clarify the major differences between the Quarto and Folio texts, in the next chapter I embark on the venture to analyse the Folio text especially its symbols, in the third part of my disquisition, I would like to present a possible kottian interpretation of the main hero, not as absurd as Jan Kott suggested, but also not classical, being thrown into the ontical space, becoming thus the deconstructed emblem of a king and a father. In addition to this I will refer to biblical allusions and clear references, and draw the attention to the complexity of character and emblems.

The method

The method I tried to use while writing this paper is inductive, trying to use excerpts of both Quarto and Folio texts in order to support my views, especially preferring Folio over Quarto and giving an ample interpretation of the figure of the Folio Lear which might be considered not so closely connected to the main goal of this dissertation, as it is not lamenting on the text instead characterizing the main hero from a post-modern point of view. This I also added to the first two chapters as I did not want that my disquisition be bereft of interpretation and contain only data of typography and editorial framework.

---

2 DOUGLAS A. BROOKS, *"King Lear" (1608) and the Typography of Literary Ambition Author(s)*. Source: Renaissance Drama, 1999-2001, New Series, Vol. 30, Institutions of the Text (1999-2001), p. 134.

Structure

The structure of my work has three main pillars. The Introduction part is the first chapter as it differentiates two considerably different sources, and talks about the abundant editorial work made on *King Lear* since Shakespeare. The Second Chapter is listing some emblems and symbols found in the text, while the Third Chapter is a genuine interpretation of Folio Lear resembling Jan Kott's *Shakespeare Our Contemporary* but not copying it, nor being restricted to this work solely.

Goal

The aim I started this work is mainly the thirst of knowledge to obtain a clear picture of the different versions of *King Lear*, and instead of accepting what is in the curriculum, trying to find out which was the original in the Shakespeare canon.

From Quarto to Folio

We would argue that the majority of the changes made from the Quarto to the Folio represent alternations to the dramatic action and characters that improve the play theatrically. There is an entire scene (4.3) in the Quarto that does not appear in the Folio. This scene, which involves Kent and a Gentleman discussing the states of mind of both Cordelia and Lear, was seen as superfluous.

But cutting the play's length is not the only change between the Quarto and the Folio. The changes include hundreds of small variants, involving words or phrases as well as full lines. Some speeches have been given to different characters, stage directions have been altered, as has punctuation. There are roughly 285 lines in the Quarto that are not in the Folio and 115 lines in the Folio that are not in the Quarto. This is clearly not just an issue of the play's running time.

The changes affect characterization, structure, emphasis and the pacing of scenes, rather than presenting radical alterations to the plot. In particular, as Michael Warren has convincingly argued, Albany and Kent are weaker characters in the Folio and Edgar's character becomes more forceful, justifying the shift to Edgar as the heir apparent for the next generation.

The best illustration of the changes from the Quarto to the Folio is perhaps the last scene of the play in which both Lear's final lines are changed and the final speech is attributed to a different character. The following passages show both a shift in King Lear's final vision of the world and a softening of the character of Kent.

Quarto text

Lear And my poor fool is hanged. No, no life?
Why should a dog, a horse, a rat have life, [280]
And thou no breath at all? O, thou wilt come no more,
Never, never, never.
Pray you, undo this button. Thank you, sir.

O, O, O, O.

Edgar He faints. My lord, my lord!
Lear Break, heart, I prithee break.
Edgar Look up, my lord.
Kent Vex not his ghost. O, let him pass. He hates him
That would upon the rack of this tough world
Stretch him out longer. [*Lear dies*]

Folio Text

Lear And my poor fool is hanged. No, no, no life?
Why should a dog, a horse, a rat have life, [280]
And thou no breath at all? Thou'lt come no more,
Never, never, never, *never, never.*
Pray you, undo this button. Thank you, sir.
Do you see this? Look on her! Look, her lips.
Look there, look there. [He dies]
Edgar He faints. My lord, my lord!
Kent Break, heart, I prithee break.
Edgar Look up, my lord.
Kent Vex not his ghost. O, let him pass. He hates him
That would upon the rack of this tough world
Stretch him out longer. [*Lear dies*]

In the above example, Lear acquires two new lines in the Folio before he dies: 'Break, heart, I prithee break'. This line is instead given to Kent, emphasising that he too has come to the end of his journey, thereby justifying the fact that he declines the opportunity to lead after Lear's death. The reintroduction of hope in Lear's last line can be either redemption and absolution or delusion.

Is there a possibility to get enlightened about the original version of the drama or is it merely the reminiscences of these copies that we have to remain content with? The "Two Versions" theorists claim that Shakespeare revised the Quarto in 1610; no evidence supports this belief, and the so-called "revisions" are entirely cuts. The Folio *Lear* contains no new scenes or characters, no rearrangements of plot, no new speeches. If Shakespeare had revised the play, many have thought, he would surely have added new words, as he did in surviving cases of revision (in *Love's Labour's Lost* and *Romeo and Juliet*). De Grazia endorses the revisionists' feeble claim that Shakespeare made these cuts so as "to accelerate the play's action" – saving only a few minutes of performance time. In fact, the cuts damage the play on several levels. They omit details essential to the action. Kent sends an anonymous (sorry, not "eponymous") Gentleman to find Cordelia and deliver a message to her; but Folio omits the earlier part of the speech telling him where to find her.

As Brooks suggests: The I6O8 quarto text of Lear has generated a more contentious critical reception than perhaps any other extant early modern playtext. Initially disparaged by textual scholars because of its hypothesised distance from Shakespeare's authorship, Q Lear' s reputation has suffered over the past thirty years because of its hypothesised proximity to the author. In the first critical scenario, the theatre, embodied by the actor who allegedly reconstructed the play from his memory, is held responsible for Q Lear' s "badness". Referring to the generalised origins of this theory, Laurie E. Maguire observes, "The response to the New Bibliography was enthusiastic . . . a specific focus of praise was the identification of suspect texts as memorial reconstructions by actors . . . Whereas before [the new bibliography] we had memorial reconstruction by diverse agents for the purposes of publication, now we had memorial reconstruction by actors for performance." As we shall see later in this chapter, Q Lear would for a time "benefit" from this theoretical "advance." In the more recent critical scenario, the theatre, embodied this time by Shakespeare himself and what he had learned from his experience of the play on stage, is indirectly held responsible for Q Lear' s "badness." From this perspective, the folio text is perceived as a superior version of the play because Shakespeare is thought to have revised it after an earlier draft of the play had been performed. Regarding the main premise that underwrites the "two-text theory" of King Lear, T. H. Howard-Hill observes, "In Shakespeare's time, the progress of a playwright's manuscript from his pen to the playhouse made it very likely that the printed text of a play could derive from different stages in the compositional process.

The most notorious cut affects the remarkable scene (III.vi) where the demented Lear, sheltering from the storm in a hovel, imagines the two "joint stools." This scene contains are his evil daughters Goneril and Regan, and empanels a jury (the Fool and "Poor Tom") to arraign them. The Folio cuts thirty-eight lines where Lear arraigns Goneril, but includes Kent's attempt to restrain Lear's anger (which has not been represented). Nonsensically, it retains Lear summoning the second plaintiff: "Then let them anatomize Regan . . . ". Shakespeare constructed *King Lear* with unusual care, adding a subplot involving another father who cannot tell a good child from an evil one, and intertwining the two to produce the catastrophe.

Michael Best gives an ample description of the story of the text, the editorial differences which I consider inevitable to quote as below:

Both the title page of the Quarto and the entry in the Stationers' Register conveniently record the first known performance: St. Stephen's Day (26 December), 1606. It would probably have been performed earlier at the Globe. The generally agreed date of composition is some time in 1605, after an somewhat fallow period in Shakespeare's writing career; it must have been written after the publication of Samuel Harsnett's engagingly entitled *A Declaration of Egregious Popish Impostures* in 1603, since from this work Shakespeare took the names of the "fiends" Edgar, as Poor Tom, mentions. The much earlier anonymous play *The Chronicle History of King Leir* (published by our sibling organisation, the Queen's Men Editions) was printed in 1605; though somewhat dated in style it may have been revived before publication and may have been the stimulus that directed Shakespeare towards his radical rewriting and restructuring of the plot.

The second version of the play appeared in 1623 in the First Folio (F), where the title was changed to accord with the division of the Folio into the genres of comedy, history, and tragedy: "THE TRAGEDIE OF KING LEAR" (Folio plays have no title pages). The two versions are significantly different in more than their titles: depending on the method of counting, Q1 includes approximately 285 lines not in F, and F records about 102 lines not in Q1. In addition, there are a large number of individually varying readings in words, phrases, and speech assignments. Sonia Massai elegantly discusses the editorial history of the play, showing how varying social and ideological pressures have shaped the way editors have understood the texts ("Working"; see also Urkowitz, "'Base,'" Holderness "Introduction," and Halio *Tragedy* 65ff.). From the earliest editions to the late twentieth century editors assumed that

Shakespeare had written a single play, which for various reasons had been garbled or corrupted in the two surviving versions; there were thus general attempts to re-create what was thought to be the closest possible approximation to Shakespeare's imagined original by conflating the two editions and making more or less eclectic decisions on which variant reading to adopt.

Best draws also a conclusion based on the survival and re-edition of Quarto Lear:

Two late twentieth-century theoretical discussions significantly complicated this deceptively neat solution. As our understanding of the processes of the theatre, print shop, and the creation of theatrical manuscripts has deepened, we have become more keenly aware of the production of a work such as *King Lear* as a social and collaborative activity; a corollary of this awareness is that scholars have become increasingly interested in looking at each version as a separate snapshot of a play that was in continuing change both on stage and in varying manuscript manifestations. The most important result of this revaluation has been a sustained argument that Shakespeare himself revised the play, and that the Folio version reflects this revision. Following early work by Michael Warren ("Quarto and Folio *King Lear*") and Steven Urkowitz (*Shakespeare's Revision*), Warren and Gary Taylor published *The Division of the Kingdoms: Shakespeare's Two Versions of King Lear* (1983), a collection of essays that argued strongly that the Folio *Lear* represents a conscious revision by Shakespeare. Three years later the new Oxford *Complete Works* edited by Taylor and Stanley Wells (1986) published two separate versions of *Lear*, one based on Q1, the other on the Folio. Since this important publication the debate about the legitimacy of a conflated text has continued and has been extended to include *Hamlet*, *Troilus and Cressida*, *Othello*, and other plays where Quarto and Folio versions differ significantly. Single-text editions of Quarto and Folio texts have appeared for many plays.

Grace Ioppolo puts the case against conflating *King Lear* trenchantly:

Any edition of *King Lear* which conflates the Quarto and Folio texts, . . . produces an inconsistent treatment of themes such as war and familial conflict, a confused presentation of the play's structure and form, and, most important, a falsely conflated version of Cordelia and so many other characters, creating a counterfeit and non-Shakespearean foundation upon which only the most limited literary interpretation and meaning can be built. (*Revising* 181)

However, not all scholars agree that deconflation is desirable or even possible. Richard Knowles uses the Quarto as his base text for his monumental Variorum *King Lear* (2018, forthcoming); his views are discussed further below. Brian Vickers in *The One King Lear* argues, in a curiously polemical tirade, that *King Lear* is really a single version where even the Folio additions can be explained away; and Peter Blayney, in a generally deeply critical review of Vickers's work, reveals that he regards the Folio text as a non-Shakespearean "adaptation" of the Quarto ("Quatrat" 64, 101).

Whatever their views on the relationship between the two versions, editors of *King Lear* are being scrutinised by theorists. Ernst Honigmann points out astutely that even those editors who attempt to produce a "pure" modern text of Q1 or F end up, in effect, conflating, since they invariably use readings from the other text in their solutions to various cruxes: "Conflation appears to be unavoidable: the question is not whether to conflate or not, but rather how much to conflate" ("The New Bibliography" 87-8).

R. A. Foakes's edition for the Arden 3 series prints a conflated version with variant readings and passages from Quarto and Folio clearly indicated by small superscript letters; Barbara Mowat and Paul Werstine's Folger *Lear* uses variously shaped brackets to distinguish the origin of different readings. The most recent Norton Shakespeare (Third Edition) includes parallel texts of each version of the play, together with what the editor, Grace Ioppolo, terms a "scars-and-stitches" version—similar in way respects to the extended Folio text; the previous version, which used the separate Oxford texts for Quarto and Folio, also provided a conflated version for the sake of convenience in teaching the play.[3]

> According to The Norton Shakespeare, the play "performed at court in December 1605, was probably written and first performed somewhat earlier, though not before 1603, since it contains allusions to a florid piece of anti-Catholic propaganda published in the year: Samuel Harsnett's *Declaration of Egregious Popish Imposture.*"[4]

The Oxford editors who broke the line of publishing Quarto and Folio Lear together as cross-reference mark an important stage in the editorial tradition of the text. Gary Taylor points out: "The entire purpose of editing Q1 and F separately is to preserve the integrity of each, and such a purpose is not well served by importing revised readings into an unrevised fabric."[5]

---

3 Michael Best, Textual Introduction, The two versions of *King Lear.* At ≤https://internetshakespeare.uvic.ca/doc/Lr_TextIntro/section/The+two+versions+of+King+Lear/index.html≥ 04.02.2021.

4 The Norton Shakespeare. Tragedies. Based on the Oxford Edition. Ed. Julia Reidhead. 2nd edition. New York.

5 The Norton Shakespeare. Id: 579. Textual Note

Text and plot analysis of the Quarto and the Folio King Lear

Based upon Stuart Elden's, *The Geopolitics of King Lear: Territory, Land, Earth*[6] I endeavour to list the textual references which may add new content to the source and at the same time shed light upon the main differences of the Quarto and the Folio texts.

In the Folio edition, King Lear is one of only two plays in Shakespeare's entire work that uses the word "territory." The plural "territories" is more common, appearing in six plays in eleven separate instances. Almost all these are places where "territories" means effectively the same thing as "lands." Richard II banishes the Duke of Hereford (the future Henry IV) from his "territories . . . upon pain of life, / Till twice five summers have enriched our fields."8 Banishment from territories also occurs in Henry VI, Part II, and is threatened in As You Like It—"or turn thou no more / To seek a living in our territory"—and in Two Gentlemen of Verona. 9 In other places people are welcomed into the territories of a kingdom,10 and there is the constant threat of conquest or conflict.11 However, in Henry VI, Part II, Lord Somerset reports on the situation in France: "That all your interest in those territories / Is utterly bereft you—all is lost."12 Although this may appear to be another use of "territories" in a sense of lands, or as a battlefield fought over and surrendered, the relation of interest shows that it is not simply property or a strategic sense, but the political control of and stake in those places. This same phrasing is the one used regarding "territory" in King Lear. Lear is discussing his plans for the inheritance of his kingdom among his three daughters.[7]

Joseph Quincy Adams points out that "aside from the fact that the Folio omits something more than two hundred lines found in the Quarto, and adds approximately fifty lines (readily explained as due either to alterations in a late promptbook or to the peculiar way in which the manuscript for the Quarto was secured), and (2) that the Quarto throughout corrupts the metre, mutilates the verse-lining, and spoils the punctuation, the two texts are identical-except in one very curious respect: giving the same sentences, in the same sequence, they nevertheless exhibit a constant variation in verbal forms (has, hath; ye, you; wrote, writ) and in individual words (smite, strike; caitiff, coward; tax, task), for the most part unimportant, or at least not affecting the sense. So numerous are these minor differences that

6 Stuart Elden's, *The Geopolitics of King Lear: Territory, Land, Earth*. ≤ file:///C:/Users/orsolypl/Downloads/Elden2013-TheGeopoliticsofKingLear.pdf≥

7 Stuart Elden's, *The Geopolitics of King Lear: Territory, Land, Earth*. ≤ file:///C:/Users/orsolypl/Downloads/Elden2013-TheGeopoliticsofKingLear.pdf≥

Miss Madeleine Doran, in her recent study, The Text of "King Lear" (1931), contends that the Quarto represents Shakespeare's first hurried draft."[8]

This scholar differentiates the two texts based on the words having been used for multiple meanings by Shakespeare, eg. Heaven- sky, heaven, etc. or the choice of words and phrases in the Folio text are even more interesting as they are often merely contracted forms of full words.

As a result of the stenographers' inability to tell from the writer's notes exactly the form in which a word was spoken, scholars tend to believe that Shakespeare would tend to write the full rather than the contracted form. According to Miss Doran, in ninety-two instances he gives the full where the Folio gives the contracted form, usually, as in the following examples to the injury of the metre:

By her is poison'd; she confesses [Q. hath confessed] it.

Sir, I love [Q. do love] you more than words can wield the matter.

That hast this fortune on me? If thou'rt [Q. beest] noble What mean'st [Q. thou] by this? Thoud'st [Q. Thou hadst] shiver'd like...[9]

In addition to all these, regarding verbs and tenses, mainly Present Tense was being used in the following witty way. First Folio verbs are cited, secondly verbs taken out from the Quarto:

"I love, I do love; comes, came; fall, fallen; needed, needs; sleep, slept; wake, waked; declined, declining; writ, wrote; writes, writ; strucken, struck; did, hath done; prais'd, praise; tended, tends; hear, heard; heard, hear; was, is; taken, took; look'd, look; drown, drown'd; contented, content; leapt, leaps; subscribe, subscrib'd; send, is sent; make, made; stolen, stole; did challenge, had challenged; starv'd, starve; had, has; wast, art; etc."[10]

The researcher thus found many mistakes in the text, too. Hereby we will list few examples only:

Many errors are due to the failure of the stenographer to change the "primitive" forms of pronouns into the correct "derivatives": Let her who [Q. that] would be rid of him. Gods, who make them [Q.

8 Joseph Quincy Adams, *The Quarto of "King Lear" and Shorthand.* Source: Modern Philology, Nov., 1933, Vol. 31, No. 2 (Nov., 1933), pp. 135-163 Published by: The University of Chicago Press: 135.

9 Adams, id: 152.

10 Adams, id: 153.

their] honours of men's impossibilities. I am none of these [Q. this], my lord. Upon these [Q. those] eyes of thine. Sometimes his failure to guess the proper "derivative" led him into still further error: Folio: Come, your hovel! Poor fool and knave, I have . . . Quarto: Come, you hovel poor; fool and knave, I have. Folio: A plague upon you, murderers, traitors all. Quarto: A plague upon your murderous traitors all. Folio: I beseech your pardon. Quarto: I beseech you pardon me. Folio: Or your fore-vouch'd affection falls into taint. Quarto: Or you for vouch'd affections fallen.[11]

It is highly interesting to see the challenges of the two texts, how they use variants of structures, word order being in constant alternation, which makes text analysis a beautiful though demanding work. These were much likely to be revised by Shakespeare himself:

Folio: Ay, my good lord.

Quarto: Ay, good my lord.

Folio: Than doth within a dull, stale . . .

Quarto: Than doth within a stale, dull . . .

Folio: Then must we look from his age to receive.

Quarto: Then must we look to receive from his age.

Folio: I have heard him oft.

Quarto: I have often heard him.

Folio: Nuncle, give me an egg.

Quarto: Give me an egg, nuncle.

Folio: That justly think'st, and hast most rightly said.

Quarto: That rightly thinks, and hast most justly said.

11 Adams, id: 154.

Folio: Which is the justice, which is the thief?

Quarto: Which is the thief, which is the justice?

Folio: I tripped up thy heels and beat thee.

Quarto: I beat thee and tripped up thy heels.

Folio: Maugre thy strength, youth, place, and eminence.

Quarto: Maugre thy strength, place, youth, and eminence.

Folio: But I have a son, sir.

Quarto: But I have, sir, a son.

Folio: Our flesh and blood, my lord, is grown so vile.

Quarto: Our flesh and blood is grown so vile, my lord.

Folio: And bring you where both fire and food is ready.

Quarto: And bring you where both food and fire is ready.

Folio: They could not, would not.

Quarto: They would not, could not.

Folio: If ever I did hate thee.

Quarto: If I did ever hate thee.[12]

As for the language used by Shakespeare, just like other Renaissance authors he also expanded language borrowing from Latin. He makes use of the process of affixation and conversion. Eg. Lear uses "accommodated" with a prefix "un" thus explaining human fragility: "Unaccommodated man is no more but such a poor, bare, forked animal as thou art" (3.4.98-100). His usage of "un" is for

12 Cited by Adams, id: 158.

negating concepts.[13]The language of the writer does not differ much from nowadays English, merely in morphosyntactic options that he used, favouring the auxiliary "do."[14]

There are scholars who opt out of the possibility of accepting Shakespeare's texts as they are and they rather scrutinise its grammatical appropriateness or deficiencies. Thus, one wrote a journal article reflecting upon improper syntax in King Lear, which was aligned with confusing stage directions that made twentieth century's directors apply their own interpretation when staging the play.

The question of a grammar for tragedy is a complex one; for the language of theatre is more than words; it is a syntax which employs gesture, sound, music, design, colour, light, and suggestion. Tragedy is, therefore, dependent not only upon the quality of literature provided by the playwright, but also upon its corollaries: the kind of language employed in production, and the kind of inferential patterns brought by the spectator into the theatre. While the dramatic form is, in one sense, static, the theatrical form is, as Harley Granville- Barker noted, also dynamic. Theatre is, therefore, a complex possessing both permanent and ephemeral traits. It is for this reason that the great dramas are critically affected by performance. Such has been the case of Shakespeare's tragedy, King Lear, which has, perhaps, more than any other major work in Western dramatic literature, been adversely affected by the quality of theatrical language to which it has been subjected.[15]

Lamenting on the different editions of *King Lear*, Margareta de Grazia concludes:

The technology of photoduplication has been fully exploited in Michael Warren's awesome *Complete KING LEAR* 1608-1623. The play has been duplicated as four units: the 1608 quarto *True Chronicle Historie,* the 1619 quarto *True Chronicle Historie,* and the 1623 Folio *Tragedie,* and Warren's own two-in-one Parallel Texts of the first and last of these three facsimiles. Furthermore, since all but the fourth unit consist of loose rather than bound pages, the materials can be assembled into any number of additional textual units. *The Complete KING LEAR* achieves with photography what the *Globe Shakespeare* achieved with typography. As the Globe attained standard fixity in print, so the *Complete KING LEAR* has attained combinatorial diversity in photo. We know how many lines make up

13 Jonathan Hope, *Shakespeare and language* in Margarata de Grazia, The New Cambridge Companion to Shakespeare (Cambridge: Cambridge Univ. Press, 2001): 83.

14 Hope, id: 84.

15 Esther Merle Jackson, *King Lear: The Grammar of Tragedy.* Shakespeare Quarterly, Winter, 1966, Vol. 17, No. 1 (Winter, 1966), pp. 25-40 Published by: Oxford University Press.

the definitive *Globe Shakespeare*; the question cannot even be intelligibly asked of the infinitely variable Warren LEAR. In order to represent textual multiplicity, the *Complete KING LEAR* has broken out of the codex format that has dominated Western literary culture for some twelve or thirteen centuries.[16]

In the forthcoming part of the first chapter we may consider the Quarto and Folio text separately, in order to progress with the symbolic interpretations of the two texts in the second chapter and examine characters of Folio in the third chapter to be able to draw a conclusion at the end of the dissertation regarding which variant is the more authentic and which one is more readable, a literary masterpiece.

The Quarto King Lear is often considered one of Shakespeare's most puzzling plays, as S.A.Small regarded it:

King Lear commonly known as the Pide Bull Quarto (1608). It shows the traces of many attempts to improve (?) the reading of the text. Though not as 'literary' in its diction as the Folio version, it is full and rich in suggestive readings, revealing changes made by a reporter, an actor, a compositor, a press reader, a scribe, and even by the author himself. Since Charles Knight in 1841 noted that the "metrical arrangement is one mass of confusion" and Nikolaus Delius in 1874 concluded his study in the Jahrbuch "gegen die Annahme einer spàteren Revision des Dramas von Shakspere's Hand," critics have given much analytical study to its text and cannot agree on its authenticity nor on how much influence it had on the editors of the First Folio. A thorough study of the textual problem of

16 Margareta De Grazia, *The Question of the One and the Many: The Globe Shakespeare, The Complete King Lear, and The New Folger Library Shakespeare.* Source: Shakespeare Quarterly, Summer, 1995, Vol. 46, No. 2 (Summer, 1995), pp. 245- 251. P. 248. "Meanwhile the works of Shakespeare are currently being reproduced in an edition that attempts to represent the diversity of multiple-text plays without dismantling the book structure: the New Folger Library Shake- speare, edited by Barbara A. Mowat and Paul Werstine. The edition intro- duces a system of square, angled, and half brackets ([ ] ( ) r 1) to designate passages incorporated from different texts, either from early texts or from later editions. While the system is new to editing Shakespeare, it is standard II Roger Chartier, "From Codes to Screen: Trajectories of the Written Word" in Forms and Meanings: Text, Performance, and Audience from Codex to Computer, forthcoming from the Uni- versity of Pennsylvania Press. This content downloaded from 46.139.247.127 on Wed, 17 Feb 2021 09:23:45 UTC All use subject to http TOOLS 249 practice in transcribing manuscripts to indicate various irregularities: for example, words written in another hand, words deleted, words written between lines or in the margins." P. 249.

this play has recently been made by Leo Kirschbaum in his book, The True Text of "King Lear", 1945, published by The Johns Hopkins.[17]

Small laments on why there is no authentic copy of the text as in Shakespearean times manuscript circulations resulted in much different printed copies as the original. The textual problem of King Lear has been brought closer to solution by Leo Kirschbaum. He considered the publication of many vital articles on the same subject, including those of Daniel, Greg, Chambers, Van Dam, and Miss Doran, to say nothing of Nikolaus Delius and Alexander Schmidt who did the pioneer work. W. W. Greg in several studies, especially in his *"The Function of Bibliography in Literary Criticism Illustrated in a Study of the Text of King Lear,"* Neophi lologus, XVIII (1933), and in the publication: *The Editorial Problem in Shakespeare*, 1942, summarised the various issues and contentions in the problem but failed to make a final solution of the problem of the Quarto text. Miss Madeleine Doran has placed high authority on the Quarto text in her *"The Text of King Lear,"* Stanford University Publications, 1931. This estimation is rejected by Leo Kirschbaum who reduces the value of the Quarto to the category of a "bad" quarto.[18]

Alice Walker reflects upon the problematic features of the Quarto text as follows:

It is generally agreed that the Folio text of King Lear was printed from a copy of Q1 (1608) which had been corrected by collation with the prompt-book. The transmission of the manuscript from which the 1608 quarto was printed is prob- lematical. It has been held that the manuscript was based on a stenographic 'report' of the play as acted and the alternative suggestion has recently been made that the manuscript represented (like that from which Q1 of Richard III was printed) a corporate effort on the part of the actors to replace a lost prompt-book. There is undoubtedly every indication in the Lear quarto of actors' perversions and vulgarisation, and any theory of the transmission of the Q1 text must take this feature into account.[19]

She discusses the weakness of the text as for instance in II. v, a short scene of twenty odd lines, there are only four readings in which the quarto and Folio texts differ, none of them significant.[20]

---

17 S. A. Small, *THE "KING LEAR" QUARTO* in The Shakespeare Association Bulletin, October, 1946, Vol. 21, No. 4 (October, 1946), pp. 177-180 Published by: Oxford University Press Stable URL: https://www.jstor.org/stable/23675233 p.177.

18 Small, id: 179.

19 Alice Walker, *"King Lear": The 1608 Quarto* in The Modern Language Review, Jul., 1952, Vol. 47, No. 3 (Jul., 1952), pp. 376-378 Published by: Modern Humanities Research Association Stable URL: https://www.jstor.org/stable/3719025 p. 376.

20 Walker, id: 376.

As an example, she quotes twice from the quarto, the second one is Poor Tom's words which make evident that in much of the quarto text in adjacent scenes there are corrections by reference to the prompt-book which is apparent in the Folio text. In the scene before the Hovel (III. iv), for instance, over considerable stretches the Q1 and Folio texts agree as closely as in III. v:

Edg. Poore Tom, that eats the swimming frog, the tode, the tod pole, the wall-newt, and the water, that in the furie of his heart, when the foule fiend rages, eats cow-dung for sallets, swallowes the old ratt, and the ditch dogge, drinkes the greene mantle of the standing poole, who is whipt from tithing to tithing, and stock-punisht and imprisoned, who hath had three sutes to his backe, sixe shirts to his bodie, horse to ride, and weapon to weare. But mise and rats, and such small Deere, Hath beene Toms foode for seuen long yeare. Beware my follower, peace snulbug, peace thou fiend.

The only Folio variants are 'stockt, punish'd', the omission of 'had' in the phrase 'who hath had three sutes' (both generally regarded as errors), the substitution of 'Haue' for 'Hath' in the second line of the rhyme, and 'Smulkin' for 'snulbug' in the last line. If this was a 'report', then Edgar would appear to have remembered the number of his suits and shirts better than Lear remembered the terms of Kent's banishment in I. i.[21]

After these Alice Walker laments about the Oakes copy, she expresses her views as reflecting upon the bad handwriting of the one who copied the text, thus many mistakes were generated, yet there are no signs of memorial contamination:

Q 1 text is extraordinarily uneven in a very strange way. The better parts of Q 1 seem to me remarkably free from memorial contamination and they are, I think, 'good' text which can only be reconciled with the undoubtedly 'bad' text of much of Acts I-II and v. iii in one way: by supposing that the manuscript from which Q1 was printed was dictated to a scribe from an authoritative manuscript, that the reader was an actor familiar with parts of the play, and that (either from haste, laziness or over-confidence) he used his memory rather than his eyes for those parts of the play with which he was well acquainted but perforce paid more attention to his manuscript when his memory did not serve. This only will explain the paradox that what should have been most memorable, like the opening scene, is least well transmitted. Given dictation, with memorial contamination, to a scribe who was a phonetic speller, had a bad handwriting (or wrote in haste), who had no feeling for metre and was apt to misapprehend what he heard, what emerged in Q 1, printed from his manuscript, is understandable in the light of the

21 Walker, id: 377.

Folio. We cannot suppose that Okes's manuscript was, in the material sense, composite because he had the same difficulty with its bad handwriting and 'aurigular' spellings throughout. We must therefore suppose that his manuscript was written in the same hand and 'copied by the ear' throughout.[22]

In her paper published in 1952 Walker examines the Quarto omissions supposing the correction of Shakespeare's hands, and also stating that these texts were corrected in theatre since the King's Men's policy was to prevent the publication of their plays. She also considers actor's role in corrupting the text, compositor's error, or copying hurriedly, coming to the conclusion that Folio is "our best authority."[23]

Sidney Thomas notes that the pioneering work by such authors as Michael Warren, Steven Urkowitz and Gary Taylor show a radically new approach to the textual problems of King Lear, with such far-reaching implications as that the Quarto text (Qi, 1608, and its derivative Q2, 1619) and the Folio text constitute two different versions of the play, the Folio version being a deliberate and careful revision by Shakespeare himself of his earlier version of the play as represented by the Quarto. All the differences between Quarto and Folio, except for obvious compositorial errors, are therefore authorial in origin and show a significant change in characterization and dramaturgy between the two versions. In his paper *Shakespeare's Supposed Revision of King Lear* Thomas gives and analyzes examples from both texts and concludes:

But at IV.ii, the Gentleman reports to Albany that the servant was slain by Cornwall, who received his wound as he "feld him dead" (sig. H4v). These two contradictory accounts of the Servant's death are unchanged, again with only minor variations (for example, "Killes him." in place of the longer Quarto stage direction) in the Folio. Other examples can be cited. There is, to mention one, the named character Curan, who makes a brief appearance at II.i in both Quarto and Folio and then as abruptly disappears from sight for the remainder of the play. It is, however, unnecessary to multiply examples: those I have discussed, it seems to me, unmistakably suggest that whatever Folio revision there may have been has been carried out hastily and carelessly and has not achieved its presumed purpose of creating a tighter dramatic structure.[24]

---

22 Walker, id: 377.

23 Walker, id: 378.

24 Sidney Thomas, *Shakespeare's Supposed Revision of King Lear* in Shakespeare Quarterly, Winter, 1984, Vol. 35, No. 4 (Winter, 1984), pp. 506-511 Published by: Oxford University Press Stable URL: https://www.jstor.org/stable/2870184 p. 508.

Thomas quotes Gary Taylor, one of the strongest supporters of the two-text theory, that the Folio-only passages do not include new narrative material or major, structurally important incidents; they do not consist of new scenes, but of alterations, they make not the slightest change in the characterizations of Lear, Cordelia, Goneril, Regan, Cornwall, Edmund, Edgar, Kent, or Gloucester.[25]Alterations according to Thomas fall into two categories: the treatment of the war set off by the invasion from France, and the characterization of Albany. He is strongly convinced that the role of Albany in the two variants is a major difference that shall be considered:

> The case for major differences in the characterization of Albany between the two texts ("the Folio variants radically alter the pattern of his development"22) has been most fully and persuasively' argued by Urkowitz in the key chapter of his book. I cannot here engage in a point-by-point 15 S. W. Reid, "The Texts of King Lear: A Review Es- say," Shakespeare Studies, 15 (1982), 328. 16 Honigmann, p. 155. 17 Op. cit. p. 376. 18 "The War in King Lear," Shakespeare Survey, 33(1980), 27-34. 19 "Time, Place, and Politics in King Lear," Collected Papers, ed. J. C. Maxwell, p. 333. 20 The Text of "King Lear" (Stanford: Stanford Univ. Press, 1983), pp. 73-76. 21 Op. cit., p. 335. 22 Urkowitz, p. 83. discussion of Urkowitz's reasoning. However, the heart of his argument is his analysis of IV.ii and V.iii, the two scenes in which the Quarto and Folio texts diverge most markedly in their treatment of Albany. I find this analysis, despite its ingenuity and sensitivity to details of staging, fatally flawed in two respects. It ignores the possibility, in some instances the near certainty, that many of the differences between Q and F are due to corruption in the Quarto text or theatrical cuts in the Folio text, none of them necessarily attributable to Shakespeare. And it consistently exaggerates the significance of these differences for the characterization of Albany and the meaning of the play as a whole.[26]

Differentiating the two texts one may argue that both are to be considered as the masterpiece of the writer, the plot is not altered yet the topic that these describe should be analysed further. The topic or topics of the text can be listed both in the plot and subplot. First of all, we shall consider the metaphysical elements of the play. The main characters each have their own theory about their place in the world, the meaning of their existence, and the relation between man and the higher powers; the play's action is thus subjected to continuous philosophical scrutiny by those who take part in it. As Paul Delany puts it, critics have been much concerned with this intricate debate about human destiny, which is carried

25 Thomas, id: 509.

26 Thomas, id: 509.

on through the play both explicitly and by the implications of dramatic action. Ultimately, it is argued, the play makes a "statement" about life, though there has been scant agreement on what the statement is. At one pole, Bradley and the neo-Christians have claimed that the play asserts the redemptive value of suffering; at the other, Jan Kott makes of it an absurdist drama about the loss of value that anticipates the modern apotheosis of the mode in the grotesque farces of Samuel Beckett. It would be obtuse to deny the importance of this metaphysical preoccupation in King Lear; obviously the play does explore the universal significance of individual experiences of pain or loss.[27]

The second notion the play is centred upon is the social issues that it describes. The mediaeval social values and deficiencies are rated as important by Danby as the opposition of organic community and atomistic state, and the shift from one to another, which is also to be found in the text. Delany calls it a double vision when speaking about social issues by the dramatist.[28] He claims that the adherence to traditional values combined with a distaste and fear of the acquisitive, unscrupulous bourgeois values shows a class conflict in Lear's world.

The social meaning of this recurrent opposition of character types has already been explored by critics, though usually from the somewhat nostalgic viewpoint of Christian humanism. E. M. W. Tillyard, for example, defines the action of Richard II as the superseding of Richard's world of "mediaeval refinement" by the more realistic, modern-minded statesmanship of Bolingbroke.6 John F. Danby takes a similar approach to King Lear, attributing Lear's faith in "Benignant Nature" to the ordered mediaeval world view of Bacon and Hooker, while seeing in Edmund's "Malignant Nature" an anticipation of Hobbes's concept of primitive culture as a war of all against all. Danby's premises are neo- Christian rather than Marxist-he says the play "is at least as Christian as the Divine Comedy…[29]

Delany calls these characters such as they have a tragic ambiguity set in the neo capitalist economy of the Renaissance. He marks that the negative characters Edmund, Regan, and Goneril "extend their political ruthlessness to the personal realm by espousing a strict and often brutal functionalism in social life."[30]

---

27 Paul Delany, *King Lear and the Decline of Feudalism* in PMLA, May, 1977, Vol. 92, No. 3 (May, 1977), pp. 429-440 Published by: Modern Language Association Stable URL: https://www.jstor.org/stable/461706 p. 429.

28 Delany, id: 430.

29 Delany, id: 431.

30 Delany, id: 433.

The above mentioned functionalism can be added to our list of elements that have a major role in the dramatic action. Edmund's functionalism in social life, seek of power and greediness results in duplicity of assertion, how formalist critics regarded the works of Shakespeare. It was Stanley Fish who argued: "to probe ever deeper the incorrigible duplicity of assertion even as it presents itself as univocal and single."[31] He referred thus to the method Shakespeare built his characters.

Delany calls attention to the emerging puritanism, or its elements in the text: "There is a tinge of puritanism in her distaste for the moral laxity of the ancien regime-a laxity made prominent at the very start of the play by Gloucester's lustful reminiscences. Like Philo in the opening scene of Antony and Cleopatra, she sees the health of the state threatened by vice and luxury in high places."[32]

Many themes and sub-themes come to our attention, such as the negative symbolism of the will to power embodied in the king's two older daughters, the erroneous royal decision, selfishness and hunger for love, the icon of the foolish king, or even the faithful servant Kent's samples, all of which testify the fact that this time, too, Shakespeare had the wit to weave several sub-themes and motifs into the text, and he managed to incorporate them all into his drama in a beautifully curved form. It is not up to us to decide whether he intended to articulate marked social criticism in negative characters, or he wanted to weave Gloucester's personal tragedy into the text precisely to achieve a dramatic effect, but the binary opposition that lies between moral and de facto blindness extends to the whole drama.

The simple elements of storytelling make this piece easy to read and interesting, as both the quarto and the folio text can be interpreted by today's reader. For the sake of authenticity, we must mention popular words from Shakespeare, such as "hath," "adder," "countenance," "vile," which are glorious examples of the age of Shakespeare, but we could still list more of them. Both texts have similar features, we do not find significant differences in their grammatical structure, the plot is the same, with the exception of the mock trial act, which, as already mentioned, is not to be found in the folio. Therefore, we already find a conflated version in the Norton Shakespeare edition in act 5. We used several sources when writing the current dissertation, basically Norton Shakespeare, but sometimes we were reaching for Folger Shakespeare or even Arden edition, the latter for folio version.

---

31 Stanley Fish qtd in Michael Taylor, Shakespeare Criticism in the Twentieth Century (Oxford: Oxford University Press, 2001.): 94.

32 Delaney, id: 433.

Second Chapter

Symbols, concepts, metaphors in Q1 and F Lear

This chapter is an attempt to call attention to the major symbols and their possible interpretation both in Quarto and Folio Lear. Since the list can be so long as a disquisition is not enough to include it, we try to minimise and restrict ourselves to the major symbols only.

One of the first symbolic interpretations, a scholar wrote quite a few pages about is the Fool and what he represents by Shakespeare. A prominent figure to be found in most of Shakespeare's comedies and some of his tragedies has multiple interpretations. We quote here an excerpt by Robert B. Hornback:

One important context regularly overlooked by those who have examined Lear's Fool and Fool variants is the historical distinction between so-called "natural" and "artificial" fool types in Renaissance England, a distinction, according to Enid Welsford, "so often made in Elizabethan times." It may be useful to offer briefly some criteria for distinguishing between these two types, especially since artificial fools stood essentially in opposition to the thing itself, the "very fool" or "natural," whose folly was real in that it came "by nature," not by pretended artifice or art. While the natural fool was an "innocent" who was generally laughed at for mental deficiencies, the artificial fool distinguished himself and his fooling with his clever, bitter wit, as he provoked laughter at others. Whereas the natural fool was dependent, and consequently often depicted as sweet and pathetic even when unintentionally insulting, the artificial fool was characterised by his consistent and intentional bitterness. Similarly, while the natural was demonstrably irrational and so was often painstakingly characterised by disjointed logic, the artificial fool was just as clearly distinguished as rational by his ordered, and occasionally even artfully formal, or syllogistic, logic. And while the natural was most foolish in that he lacked self-knowledge, the artificial fool was, like Feste in Twelfth Night, "wise enough to play the fool" (3.1.60)8 and philosophical in that he harped upon the humanistic,

Socratically-inspired themes of noscete ipsum ("know thyself") and of the universality of folly. Finally, whereas the natural was typically an unconsciously anarchic or subversive deviant who innocently flouted customary rules and turned the world upside down, the "fool by art" regularly self-consciously flouted transgression itself, exposing the socially deviant as natural fools. Therefore, while the natural fool's humour was often carnivalesque, the artificial fool's comedy was instead typically more "normative" in character in that it mocked deviations from such norms.[33]

Beside the interpretation of the Fool, Cordelia and other symbols we shall mostly concentrate on the origin of the centaur symbol so vehemently used by Lear in his harsh outrage against his daughters; the meaning of "double blindness" with its multi-layered symbolism, versed by Shakespeare in a way that it still unparalleled in poetry.

Historically, we know about the appearances of fools or jesters in the courts of mediaeval English aristocracy already in the twelfth century. In Renaissance times, aristocratic households in Britain employed licensed fools or jesters, who sometimes dressed as other servants, but generally wore a motley (i.e. parti-coloured) coat, hood with ass ears or a red-flannel coxcomb and bells. By the time of Queen Elizabeth's reign (1558-1603), courtly fools were a common feature of English society. Under the Stuart kings their status was highly elevated. In Elizabethan times, the role of a fool was to professionally entertain others, specifically the king. They served not simply to amuse but also criticise their master or mistress and their guests. Queen Elizabeth is said to have rebuked one of her fools for being insufficiently severe with her. Excessive behaviour, however, could lead to a fool being whipped, as Lear threatens to whip his fool. The Elizabethan and Jacobean fools were primarily servants, yet, in many cases, they were much indulged. Often they were kept and liked as pets, sometimes they made ascending carriers. (Archie Armstrong, for example, was the official fool both to King James VI/I (1566-1625) and his son, King Charles I. (1600-1649). To King James, Armstrong was, in a sense, a gentleman groom of the chambers as well as a source of amusement. He was paid by the king and part of his income derived from bribes from those wishing to petition the king. Despite King James' wellknown dislike of tobacco, Archie was granted a royal patent for the manufacture of tobacco pipes. He was also made a free citizen of Aberdeen.)

---

33 Robert B. Hornback, *The Fool in Quarto and Folio "King Lear"* Source: English Literary Renaissance, AUTUMN 2004, Vol. 34, No. 3, STUDIES IN SHAKESPEARE (AUTUMN 2004), pp. 306-338 Published by: The University of Chicago Press. P. 309.

Enid Welsford[34] has an ample explanation regarding the fool's role in society as follows:

The fool or jester started in the East, arriving in ancient Greece as a joker before firmly ensconcing himself in Roman drama as a figure of fun. Though it was unclear how a mentally deficient person became an entertainer, especially during much of history when handicaps, both mental and physical, were derided. By the middle ages, a court jester was often well-treated and well-fed, and often treated as a mascot. The fool may rarely have become a high officer, but in Elizabethan and Stuart times, he was considered an abstraction, a generalised figure of chaos. The English fool, moreover, didn't evolve in isolation: the Fool in Shakespeare's King Lear bears a strong resemblance to the mediaeval French *sot.*

Fools were partly born to the job; they were misshapen or mentally-deficient individuals, or those afflicted with dwarfism. Such fools were very often considered pets – though generally much loved by their masters – and appear infrequently in Shakespeare's plays. The other category of fools, in contrast, possessed verbal wit and talent for intellectual thinking and repartee. Into this category of "wise-fools" belongs King Lear's unnamed Fool.

Scholars wrote quite a few pages about the Fool and what he represents by Shakespeare. A prominent figure to be found in most of Shakespeare's comedies and some of his tragedies has multiple interpretations. We quote here an excerpt by Robert B. Hornback:

While the natural fool was most foolish in that he lacked self-knowledge, the artificial fool was, like Feste in Twelfth Night, "wise enough to play the fool" and philosophical in that he harped upon the humanistic, Socratically-inspired themes of noscete ipsum ("know thyself") and of the universality of folly. Finally, whereas the natural was typically an unconsciously anarchic or subversive deviant who innocently flouted customary rules and turned the world upside down, the "fool by art" regularly self-consciously flouted transgression itself, exposing the socially deviant as natural fools. Therefore, while the natural fool's humor was often carnivalesque, the artificial fool's comedy was instead typically more "normative" in character in that it mocked deviations from such norms. [35]

34 Enid Welsford: *The Fool, his Social and Literary History,* 1938, Farrah and Rinehart Incorporated, On Murray Hill, New York

35 Robert B. Hornback, *The Fool in Quarto and Folio "King Lear"* Source: English Literary Renaissance, AUTUMN 2004, Vol. 34, No. 3, STUDIES IN SHAKESPEARE (AUTUMN 2004), pp. 306-338 Published by: The University of Chicago Press. P. 309.

The substitution of artificial fools such as Touchstone, Feste, Lavatch, Thersites, Carlo Buffone, and Passarello for the carnivalesque clowns that had dominated the 1580s and 1590s indicates that playwrights were self-consciously participating in a change of fashion in the years after 1599. For more than a decade thereafter the artificial fool became the most prominent comic character. Thus Shakespeare also used this figure: the Quarto Fool variants –as discussed by Hornback (id: 311.) – published in 1608 make most sense if situated within the context of the specific theatrical trend of "spin-offs" favoring the artificial fools played by Armin, while the subsequent Folio Fool is a more pitiable or pathetic natural Fool in keeping with another trend, the increasing taste for pathos already evident in Shakespeare's last plays and in the works of Beaumont and Fletcher. Shakespeare used the character of Fool to explicitly expose the truth. One character who is not integrated into the Sodom of society where Cordelia and her innocence is banished, or Edgar who is also homeless due to his bastard brother, it is only the Fool who can echo the first words of Cordelia "nothing".

For more than a decade thereafter the artificial fool became the most prominent comic character. Thus, Shakespeare also used this figure: the Quarto Fool variant published in 1608 makes most sense if situated within the context of the specific theatrical trend of "spin-offs" favoring the artificial fools played by Armin, while the subsequent Folio Fool is a more pitiable or pathetic natural Fool in keeping with another trend, the increasing taste for pathos already evident in Shakespeare's latest plays and in the works of Beaumont and Fletcher."

The dramatic sources of Shakespeare's simple-minded clowns are at least as old as classical antiquity. In the plays themselves, such figures as Bottom of *A Midsummer Night's Dream* and Dogberry of *Much Ado About Nothing* are typically classified as clowns, their principal function being to arouse the mirth of audiences.

The jester played a dynamic and changing role in entertaining aristocratic households in a wide variety of ways: songs, music, storytelling, mediaeval satire, physical comedy and, to a lesser extent, juggling and acrobatics. Shakespeare not only borrowed from this multi-talented jester tradition, but contributed significantly to its rethinking. Whereas the court jester often regaled his audience with various skills aimed to amuse, Shakespeare's fool, consistent with Shakespeare's revolutionary ideas about theatre, became a complex character who could highlight more important issues. Like Shakespeare's other characters, the fool began to speak outside of the narrow confines of exemplary morality. Shakespeare's fools address themes of love, psychic turmoil, personal identity, and many other innumerable themes that arise in Shakespeare, and in modern theatre.

Another approach of the profession of the jester shows it as ambiguous, abounding in internal contradictions, arising out of the discrepancy between profession and philosophy. The profession of a jester is to provide entertainment. His philosophy demands him to tell the truth and abolish myths. The Fool in *King Lear* does not even have a name, he is just a Fool, pure Fool. But he is the first fool to be aware of the fool's position:

Fool: I marvel what kin thou and thy daughters are.
They'll have me whipped for speaking true; thou'lt
have me whipped for lying, and sometimes I am
whipped for holding my peace. I had rather be any
kind o'thing than a fool. And yet I would not be
thee, nuncle" (Act 1, Scene 4, 186-91)[36]

Fools were pampered and allowed some licence when 'entertaining' their masters. It is shown by the lines at the beginning of *King Lear,* where Lear calls the Fool "my pretty knave" (Act 1, Scene 4, 98), yet also threatens him with a beating "Take heed, sirrah–the whip" (Act 1, Scene 4, 114). And the Fool may call Lear 'nuncle': "How now, nuncle?" (for example in Act 1, Scene 4, 108). Nonetheless the Fool's criticism of Lear's lack of foresight is often particularly trenchant and yet tolerated:

Fool: When thou
clovest thy crown i' th' middle and gav'st away
both parts, thou bor'st thine ass on thy back o'er
the dirt. Thou hadst little wit in thy bald crown
when thou gav'st thy golden one away
(Act 1, Scene 4, 163-167).37

The thematic function of these peculiar individuals, the Shakespearean clowns and fools, has been largely explored by critics. Many commentators have observed the satirical potential of the fool. Considered an outcast to a degree, the fool was frequently given reign to comment on society and the actions of his social superiors; thus, some Shakespearean fools demonstrate a subversive potential. They

36 All quotation in this sub-chapter from now on from https://shakespeare.folger.edu/shakespeares-works/king-lear/

37 Folger Shakespeare. The History of King Lear.

may present a radically different worldview than those held by the majority of a play's characters, as critic Roger Ellis (1968) has observed.

Likewise, such figures can be construed as disrupting the traditional order of society and the meaning of conventional language, as Roberta Mullini (1985) has argued. As for so-called clowns —including the simple "mechanicals" of *A Midsummer Night's Dream,* Trinculo of *The Tempest,* and Launcelot Gobbo of *The Merchant of Venice* — most are thought to parody the actions of other characters in the main plots of their respective plays and to provide low humor for the entertainment of groundlings (people who could not afford to pay for seats in the theatre).

Other topics of critical inquiry concerning fools are varied. Several scholars have studied the significance of certain Elizabethan actors who were thought to have initially enacted the roles Shakespeare wrote. Preeminent among these is the comedic actor Robert Armin, for whom, as several critics have suggested, Shakespeare created the witty, even philosophical, fool roles of Feste, Touchstone, and Lear's Fool.

Still other critics have focused on Shakespeare's less easily categorised clowns. Walter Kaiser (1963) has examined Falstaff's multifaceted function in the *Henriad,* which he has argued bears similarities to those of Shakespeare's other "wise fools." William Willeford (1969) focused on the darker side of folly by exploring the title character of *Hamlet* as a unique form of the Shakespearean fool. Additionally, Catherine I. Cox (1992) investigated Shakespeare's characteristic blending of comedy and tragedy through the use of clowns and other purveyors of laughter in his tragic plays.

The main features of the all-licensed Fool in King Lear

The fool *speaks out* the truth. The Fool acts as a commentator on events and is one of the characters (Kent being the other) who is fearless in speaking the truth. The Fool provides wit and humour to the rather bleak play, and unlike some of Shakespeare's clowns who seem unfunny to us today because their topical jokes no longer make sense, the Fool in *King Lear* ridicules Lear's actions and situation in such a way that audiences of any time understand the point of his jokes.

The fool *sees* straight to the heart of the matter. His 'mental eye' is the most acute in the beginning of the play: he sees Lear's daughters for what they are and has the foresight to see the outcome. Lear's love test and division of the kingdom is based on vanity and lack of foresight. The Fool sees this and comments on it immediately, saying Lear is the one who should be fool: "All thy other titles thou hast given away; that thou wast born with" (Act 1, Scene 4, 153-154).[38] He is aware of Goneril and Regan's true nature and the danger they pose: "The hedge-sparrow fed the cuckoo so long / That it had its head bit off by it young" (Act l, Scene 4, 221-221).[39] He offers his coxcomb "For taking one's part that's out of favour . . . If thou follow him, thou must needs wear my coxcomb" (Act 1, Scene 4, 102,107).[40]

One striking point of the Fool is that he doesn't behave or speak like other people; this makes it hard to account for him in normal terms. Lear's Fool calls the king 'nuncle' and is addressed as 'boy', perhaps suggesting the kind of innocence associated with the 'natural' Fool; however, he also calls Lear 'my boy' (Act 1, Scene 4, 141)[41] and it is possible to read the generational language as satiric irony. Either way, the fool provides an alternative perspective on the king's behaviour, one that isn't bound by the political deference to which other courtiers are expected to conform. He has a privileged role in a play where characters who speak to the king with honesty instead of self-interested flattery are cast out as Cordelia and Kent.

The Fool *acts* as a kind of chorus. He shows the audience that Lear is unwise: "If I gave them all my living, I'd keep my coxcombs myself" (Act 1, Scene 4, 111-112).[42] He is a symbol of truth in a world of lies and deceit: "Truth's a dog must to kennel; he must be whipped out, when Lady Brach may stand by the fire and stink" (Act 2, Scene 4, 115-117).[43]

The Fool is the only character that is permitted to tell Lear the truth. Although the Fool does not hold an important position in court, unlike Kent for example, the Fool is allowed to criticise Lear and avoid punishment protected by his low but privileged status.

The Fool represents unstinting love and loyalty to his master. His criticisms are meant as help: he endeavours to show Lear the foolishness of his actions: "Thou shouldst not have been old till thou hadst been wise" (Act 1, Scene 5, 43-44).[44] The Fool stays with Lear through his time on the heath in the storm. He says: "...the Fool will stay, / And let the wise man fly" (Act 2, Scene 4, 88-89). He tries to

38 Folger Shakespeare. The History of King Lear.
39 Folger Shakespeare. The History of King Lear.
40 Folger Shakespeare. The History of King Lear.
41 Folger Shakespeare. The History of King Lear.
42 Folger Shakespeare. The History of King Lear.
43 Folger Shakespeare. The History of King Lear.
44 Folger Shakespeare. The History of King Lear.

persuade Lear to take shelter, even if it means returning to Gloucester's castle: "Good nuncle, in, and ask thy daughters' blessing" (Act 3, Scene 2, 13-14).[45]

The Fool provides some relief by his humour. When Lear marvels at Tom O'Bedlam's lack of clothing (he is clad only in a blanket) and wonders if the beggar's ungrateful daughters could have brought him to this pass, the Fool wryly observes: "Nay, he reserved a blanket, else we had been all shamed" (Act 3, Scene 4, 71-72).[46] He ridicules Lear's actions in such a way that his humour remains relevant.

In general, the Fool's character coincides with the convention in Shakespearean time, i.e.: The fool is a gifted individual who has an intuitive response to difficult situations and is far from foolish. It succeeds where intellect fails: good and evil are not battles of the mind, but of the soul.

As Isaac Asimov[47] wittily remarked of all 'artificial' fools: "That, of course, is the great secret of the successful fool – that he is no fool at all."Another interesting approach to the Fool's nature and psychology is presented by Melving Seiden in his essay written about the fool and Edmond.[48] "Lear's past life, though hardly mentioned, can be inferred, at least in broad line from the "data" given in the play. The King has been somewhere and been something; he is now journeying elsewhere and will become different from what he has been; he has a past, a personal history. For him, as for all of us time makes itself felt in the interplay of was, is and will–be.

With the Fool one has the sense of him being out of time, without a past, miraculously free of the weight of experience. Like a god, the Fool has come full blown onto the world; he is fated never to have been or to become of anything or anyone other than he eternally is.

The fool is man-like, boy-like, sage-like, and idiot-like; but he is not unequivocally a man, a boy, a sage, and idiot; and no one can fail to perceive this troublesome and disorienting fact about him. Uncorrupted and incorruptible, the Fool, insofar as he is a person at all, he is both less and more than a human.

The fundamental difference between the Fool of King Lear and Shakespeare's other clowns that the others carry with them an individuating signature of their personal history, Lear's Fool doesn't.

---

45 Folger Shakespeare. The History of King Lear.

46 Folger Shakespeare. The History of King Lear.

47 Isaac Asimov, American literary critic and writer

48 Seiden, Melvin. "*The Fool and Edmund: Kin and Kind.*" Studies in English Literature*, 1500-1900*, vol. 19, no. 2

The Fool embodies irreconcilable contradictions, the central one being the supra-logical phenomenon wherein the Fool is both fool and wise man; he is also rational and irrational, young and old, principled and unscrupulous, bawdy and chaste, friend and foe to his master, the King, and an object of ridicule and of pathos.

As Melvin Seiden puts it:

With the Fool one has the sense of his being out of time, without a past, miraculously free of the weight of experience. Like a god the Fool has come full blown into the world; he is fated never to have been or to become anything or anyone other than what he eternally is. The Fool incarnates the stasis of Being impervious to the flux of Becoming. We cannot relate the human aspects of the Fool to his choric or gnomic utterances. Like Keats's urn, the Fool is a mystery, not, to be sure, a silent but a perfect form that "dost tease us out of thought / As doth eternity." The mystery is a function of his uniqueness; it is an ontological mystery.[49]

The Fool being a mystery can be related to transcendence, he is considered a supernatural figure by Seiden (id. 198.), uncorrupted and incorruptible, his "ontological status" reverberates Aristotle's character theory: "Thus as Aristotle defines it, "character" is conceived of as a conceptual means of arresting the experiential flux of behaviour into a fixed, unchanging idea: the Platonic reduction of the multifariousness of a life being lived to an idea that converts contradic- tion and chaos into coherence and form."[50] Therefore Seiden argues that he "carries with him the individuating signature of a personal history."[51] The Fool in King Lear has "licence to tease, cajole, and scourge his master is a power to usurp regal power and privilege."[52] Seiden's further ideas relate to the verbal pictures the Fool projects:

"...projecting verbal pictures not of his own making. The Fool is only the medium through which these images are expressed. Personally (if it is possible to speak of the Fool as a person), he neither enjoys nor is disgusted by these images; he does not judge them; he does not take a moral position in respect to, let us say, the work of the organ housed in the codpiece. Yet neither is the Fool the objective reporter;

49 Melvin Seiden, *The Fool and Edmund: Kin and Kind.* Studies in English Literature, 1500-1900, Spring, 1979, Vol. 19, No. 2, Elizabethan and Jacobean Drama (Spring, 1979), pp. 197-214 Published by: Rice University Stable URL: https://www.jstor.org/stable/450204 p. 197-198.

50 Aristotle qtd in Seiden, id: 199.

51 Seiden, id: 199.

52 Seiden, id: 200.

he is not saying, as Edmund the natural scien- tist might say: Men and women "make love" just as and for the same reasons that animals couple. After all, that's what they-we-are: animals."

Seiden calls this drama a "comedy of castration to an old, beaten, and impotent man" [53]where the Fool is a supra-logical phenomenon, irrational and wise, paradoxical, "the only major character in the play who has no family ties."[54]

One slight interpretation shall be made on the notion of "nothing" used by Cordelia in 1.1, later by the Fool while talking to the king. Since Seiden points out the major importance of this word so professionally, we quote here his approach briefly:

Lear criticism, notably in the brilliantly imaginative writing of the late Sigurd Burckhardt, has explored the rich vein of meanings which may be discovered in these bland nothings containing the somethings of Tragedy.9 It is not necessary to mine this ground again. A new insight emerges, however, if we see the Fool as the living embodiment 9Sigurd Burckhardt, "King Lear: The Quality of Nothing," Shakespearean Mean- ings (Princeton: Princeton Univ. Press, 1968). Burckhardt ends his essay with a medi- tation on "nothing": "There can be honesty in speaking what we feel, but what we ought to say is the naked truth, and it cannot be said. "Make 'nothing' into a substance, and you get Nothing; take it for a mere sign, and you have 'nothing.' Be king or subject -nothing will be the sum of your earnings. But the uncompromis- ing logic - the logic of life and language, not of syllogisms- with which we work out or more likely let ourselves be led to this sum is, perhaps, some- thing." (p. 259) of this paradox: he is now linked symbolically-organically- to death in its most vivid manifestation -one is tempted to spin yet another paradox, to speak of Death in its most living form: Cordelia, "dead as earth," (V. iii. 261) a dead weight in her father's arms, a voice that has been silenced. "What is't thou say'st?" Lear asks, imagining that she has spoken (V. iii. 272). She has said nothing; but we can remember when she said: "Nothing, my lord" (I. i. 89). If we remember that nothing, then we must also remember the Fool. In the first scene in which he appears the Fool puts to the king a cruel question which reveals the credentials of the questioner: "Can you make no use of nothing, Nuncle?" (I. iv. 143). Walking into the same trap of blind literalism he had built for himself in negotiating treaties of love with his daughters, Lear answers the Fool with words that echo his earlier reply to Cordelia's "Nothing": "Nothing can be made out of nothing" (I. iv. 145). To Cordelia Lear had said, "Nothing can come of nothing" (I. i. 92); there is a subtle difference worth noticing in the shift in the second response to the phrase, can be made out of: the first is passive, the second active.

53 Seiden, id: 202.

54 Seiden, id: 204.

All these lead us to the conclusion that the verbal frame Shakespeare used in the utterances of the characters contribute to the sublime absurd symbolism that shall be listed in the Third Chapter of this disquisition, all like the symbol of the storm, reflect nihilism, the loss of God and hope, "nothing" being the notion of the twentieth century absurd drama, and that of the non existence, the reduction of the self.

How the Quatro and Folio Versions Reflect on Fool Interpretations

We have already discussed in general the differences between the Quatro and Folio versions of *King Lear* in the First Chapter of this disquisition. We have introduced the most noted views by scholars on the differences between the Quatro and Folio Fool, the natural and artificial. Now we endeavour to throw some light on this subject by pointing out the most important deviations between the two texts concentrating on the lines spoken by the Fool.

The Folio text entirely cuts the mock trial scene in 3.6. The mock trial is spectacular evidence of Lear's madness in the Quarto, since he wants to bring justice to persons he himself can only see. The fool bitterly calls attention to the transgressive irrationality of Lear's raving about the imaginary defendant, Goneril, when he refuses to see what Lear sees:

Lear: "Arraign her first. T'is Goneril: I here take my oath
before this honourable assembly she kicked the poor
King his father.
Fool: Come hither, mistress. Is your name Goneril?
Lear: She cannot deny it.
Fool: Cry you mercy. I took you for a joint-stool
(Q 3.6.50-55).[55]

The final line of this Quatro-only exchange, the Fool's last line in the Quarto text, shows his refusal to humouring the mad Lear. The last line in the Folio variant, that makes the Fool most typically a pitiable natural, is the poignant, enigmatic statement, "And I"ll go to bed at noon (F-only Act 3, Scene 6, 90). It is the Fool's response to the mad Lear's inversionary claim: "we'll go

55 Folger Shakespeare. The History of King Lear.

to supper in the morning" (Act 3.Scene 6, 89). Not only does the Fool acquiesce to Lear's inversion of custom, but he also identifies pathetically with a flower that shuts itself away after the passing away of the noon-day sun. The allusion suggests the Folio Fool's resignation: since the failing King will not return to glory, the Fool will also "shew…not his face" again. While a bitter interpretation of the line is certainly possible, for those familiar with the allusion, as a Jacobean audience would have been, the line cannot be so easily separated from its pathetic undertones. The presupposition that the Folio Fool must be an "enhanced" version of the supposedly less bitter Quatro Fool has led textual scholars to read the Folio-only line as a "mocking exit line" or as an expression of the Fool's determination to leave *King Lear* with its course half run. But the death or abandonment is difficult to justify, since in Quatro the scene concludes with Kent's commanding the Fool, "Come on, help to bear your master / Thou must not stay behind (Q. Act 3, Scene 6, 107-109). Kent's command may suggest here that the Quarto Fool is not only not dying, but may actually be acting out of self-interest, trying to stay behind to detach himself from Lear's company. This detachment would be within the powers of an artificial fool capable of independence and self-sufficiency. The Folio implied abandonment of the Fool is certainly effective dramatically, precisely because its emphatically shivering Fool seems either to be dying, or to be an utterly, pathetically dependent natural unable to care for himself.

But it is not how the line has usually been interpreted in performance. When the Fool was first restored to stage in 1838 following his editorial excision by Nahum Tate in 1681, the Fool in *King Lear* has been more than an enigma. The pathos of a sweet, natural fool consistently derives from the Folio text, while the Fool in the Quarto is a funnier, wiser, and more bitter artificial fool.

The Quarto's Fool is recognizably an artificial fool when he bitterly pursues an attack on Lear's folly in several lines which the Folio text omits entirely. In the Quarto text the Fool answers his riddle, "Dost know the difference, my boy, between a bitter fool and a sweet one? (Q Act 1, Scene 4, 142-32) prompted by Lear's "No lad, teach me" (Q Act1, Scene 4, 143), the Quarto Fool begins a famous exchange with Lear which appears only in Quarto text:

Fool: That Lord that counselled thee
To give away thy land,
Come, place him here by me;
Do thou for him stand.

The sweet and bitter fool
Will presently appear:
The one in motley here,
The other found out there.
Lear: Dost thou call me fool, boy?
Fool: All your other titles thou hast given away;
that you wast born with.
Kent: This is not altogether fool, my lord.
Fool: No, faith, lords and great men will not let me. If
I had a monopoly out, they would have part on't;
and ladies too: they will not let me have all the fool
to myself; they will be snatching (Q Act 1, Scene 4, 143-55).[56]

The Fool believes that Lear's foolish decision has turned the world topsy-turvy by reversing power and status: "When thou clovest thy crown i' th' middle and gav'st away both parts, thou borest thine ass o' th' back ov'r the dirt" (Q Act 1. Scene 4, 163-166); "[…thou mad'st thy daughters they mother …when you gav'st them the rod… and putt'st down thy own breeches" (Q Act 1, Scene 4, 176-78); and „May not an ass no when the cart draws the horse? (Q Ac t 1, Scene 4, 229-30).

"King Lear and Homelessness" is an essay written by Emma Whipday in 2019, published in *Shakespeare's Domestic Tragedies, Violence in Early Modern Home*[57] which reflects upon a modern phenomenon, namely "homelessness" to be found by Shakespeare already. She contrasts homes that are places of safety with the court where Lear is "refused to entry to the hoped- for refuge" whereas parallel in the subplot "Edmund treacherously invites Edgar to 'retire with me to my lodging…there's my key."[58]The researcher leads us to the idea that the notion of "home" is a myth to be explored. She concludes: "The characters in this play are adrift from the world of domestic tragedy, but Lear shares the interest in the relationship between household hierarchy and personal identity that is characteristic of the other plays discussed in this book."[59]

---

56 Folger Shakespeare. The History of King Lear.

57 Emma Whipday, *Shakespeare's Domestic Tragedies, Violence in Early Modern Home* (Cambridge: Cambridge University Press, 2019): 203-223.

58 Whipday, id: 206.

59 Whipday, id: 206.

In the line of emblems and metaphors, we should not neglect the Christian tradition that gave new perspectives both to text analysis and character interpretation. The so-called classic *King Lear and the Gods* by William R. Elton mentions several works from *Redemption of King Lear* onwards, where Christ himself is envisioned in tragic character, see Wilson Knight: "Shakespearean tragic hero is a miniature Christ."[60] He discusses Geoffrey L. Bickersteth's statement, Cordelia as part of Christ.[61] Paul N. Siegel even goes further with the allegory of redemption as follows:

This miracle is the redemption of Lear for heaven, a redemption analogous to the redemption of mankind, for which the Son of God had come down to earth. The analogy between Cordelia and Christ, who redeemed human nature from the curse brought on it by Adam and Eve, is made unmistakable, although not crudely explicit...Cordelia's ignominious death completes the analogy between her and Christ....The "brand of heaven"...in releasing their (Cordelia's and Lear's) souls from the prison of their bodies, enabled them to become reunited in eternal bliss.[62]

It is also William R. Elton who laments about the microcosmic suffering in *King Lear* as a punishment by God, he says in the "Dantean sense comic, the macrocosm too, has a corollary orderliness."[63]

Modern criticism of King Lear has emphasised that it is the most meta- physical of Shakespeare's tragedies. The main characters each have their own theory about their place in the world, the meaning of their existence, and the relation between man and the higher powers; the play's action is thus subjected to continuous philosophical scrutiny by those who take part in it. Critics have been much concerned with this intricate debate about human destiny, which is carried on through the play both explicitly and by the implications of dramatic action. Ultimately, it is argued, the play makes a "statement" about life, though there has been scant agreement on what the statement is. At one pole, Bradley and the neo-Christians have claimed that the play asserts the redemptive value of suffering; at the other, Jan Kott makes of it an absurdist drama about the loss of value that anticipates the modern apotheosis of the mode in the grotesque farces of Samuel Becket.[64]

---

60 Knight qtd in William R. Elton, *King Lear and the Gods* (The University Press of Kentucky,1988): 3.

61 *The Golden World of King Lear,* Annual Shakespeare Lecture of the British Academy, XXXII (1946), 26.

62 *Shakespearean Tragedy and the Elizabethan Compromise* (New York, 1957). pp. 185-186.

63 Elton, id: 5.

64 Paul Delany, *King Lear and the Decline of Feudalism* Source: PMLA, May, 1977, Vol. 92, No. 3 (May, 1977), pp. 429-440 Published by: Modern Language Association Stable URL: https://www.jstor.org/stable/461706

A new theorist claims similar views on *King Lear* reception as Elton's biblical interpretation. "King Lear" and Chaos by L. M. STOROZYNSKY discusses symbolism as follows:

Mythological and biblical stories about the creation of the world from Chaos provide an informing principle in King Lear. Such narratives familiar to Elizabethans include Hesiod's Theogony, Ovid's Metamorphoses, and the book of Genesis.1 A characteristic feature of these narratives is a cyclical pattern of creation followed by destruction and the return to a state of chaos. Moreover, in classical and biblical accounts of creation, while harmony among the elements that make up the world is the desired end, it is achieved only through their division or separation. King Lear has been called 'a play about the end of the world,'2 but it is also a story of creation and destruction, and especially of separation and division. But, whereas in the earlier myths the very world is born of Chaos- of the void- of nothing- central to the play is Lear's assertion that 'Nothing can come of nothing' (1.82),3 an expression recognisable to Elizabethans as both a commonplace saying, and a controversial doctrine, ex nihilo nihil fit, denying creation.[65]

Paul Delany in his essay focuses mostly on first quarto of *King Lear* (1608), called *"True Chronicle Historie"* (i.e., a play based on matter from Holinshed or other early chronicles) and that it has much in common with Shakespeare's earlier works in the genre, especially the tetralogy that begins with Richard II. He claims that *King Lear* represents the neo capitalist economy of the Renaissance, not directly, but rather through an exploration of the philosophical concepts and moral values that are typically associated with that economy. He lists a few examples of the text which will be discussed in the third chapter of this current wor

For Gloucester, "the bond crack'd 'twixt son and father" (I.ii.113) is but one symptom of a general disorder: "in cities, mutinies; in countries, discord; in palaces, trea- son." That he should blame it all on "late eclipses in the sun and moon" (I.ii.106) merely shows his ignorance of the real forces of change at work in the kingdom. There is a similarly ironic ignorance in Lear's loss of insight and control in the division scene: he is seduced by Goneril's rhetoric, which denies all order and limit in claiming to love him "Dearer than eye- sight, space and liberty," whereas he scorns Cordelia's modest pledge to love him "Accord- ing to [her] bond; no more nor less" (i.i.56, 93). For Edmund the word has an opposite meaning: the individual's obligations to society he brushes aside as no more than "the plague of custom" (I.ii.3).

65 L. M. STOROZYNSKY, *"King Lear" and Chaos Critical Survey* Vol. 3, No. 2 (1991), pp. 163-169

The notion of bond and bound has a double symbolic meaning, the tight familiar relationships being in binary opposition of Edmund's bonds, the corrupted social bond.

Simon Palfrey calls our attention to the symbol of "banishment" and "nakedness." He argues that banishment its condition and structure is a sort of "structure of sovereignty" in a paradoxic model as "there is nothing outside the law:"[66]"whereas banishment grants the fact of exile a curious legal status, gives to homelessness and itinerance a certain supracitizenship, Edgar is simply running."[67]

Considering Edgar's so Poor Tom's soliloquy, Palfrey notes that the usage of verbs are not random, but have a double meaning, so "presented" partly withdraws the ultimacy of "nakedness": it is in part a show, a pantomime of self-reduction. Likewise, "out-face" is both a verb (to defy, rebuke, outlast) and a noun (the countenance outside in the elements). The pun suggests a man watching himself debase himself, mordant about life's strange turns, he will indeed be subject to unusual vigilance."[68] At the very last paragraph of his chapter *Into the Hollow* he chooses to discuss the notion of "mortify", according to his views this word is crucial as it suggests the humiliated body that is ashamed and suffering, as we can closely see in Edgar's behaviour, while he is reducing himself to a "horrible object", he is really rehearsing "self-erasure" and so "passing into non-being."[69] Here we may connect to the kottian absurd interpretation, but this will be discussed in the third chapter where an ample investigation is being made about the absurd symbolism found in the Folio text of *King Lear.*

In addition to this we shall consider the explicit symbols offered by Shakespeare himself. The map is the next symbol that is exposed already in the very first scene. The connection between the king and the land is incorporated in a de facto object:

This ritualistic exchange of filial love for property depends upon the map as a fetish for kingly authority. As one reader has recently noted, "the appearance of the map confirms the royal power to administrate and allocate space."4 If Lear's will is to divide the kingdom into three parts, it is more than successful, for the tearing of the map initiates a tragic calculus of division and dissolution that will continue until the play ends with Lear and his daughters propertyless in every sense. Betraying the exchange of affection for property, Lear's command, "the map there," is a gesture that will achieve tragic

66 Simon Palfrey, *Poor Tom, Living King Lear.* (Chicago: University of Chicago Press, 2014): 29-30.

67 Palfrey, id:30.

68 Palfrey, id: 31.

69 Palfrey, id: 32-33.

fulfilment in the last act, when the bereft father gives the futile command, "Look there, look there!" (5.3.309). In the end, there will be no there there-only Cordelia's corpse.[70]

Dan Brayton calls it a test of love, a cartographic ritual. His essay focuses mainly on banishment, social dissolution, the connection between geography and aristocratic identity, and he believes that Lear's ritual situates the female body at the site of anxieties about the transmission of property.[71] Brayton also notes that Halpern's ideas shall be quoted reflecting on Lear's hysteria: What does Lear suffer from: hysteria or historia? Is the play to be read in a psychoanalytic, ethical, and personal register or in a political and historical one? Both approaches are partially satisfactory, neither fully so; both leave a residue that resists critical totalization. Like hysterica/historica, two terms fighting for the same textual space, each mode of reading has a certain claim to legitimacy, and neither manages fully to supplant or eradicate the other.11 Halpern identifies in Lear scholarship the spatial agon that is at the heart of the play itself, that of "two terms fighting for the same space."

King Lear and what he represents

The Old Age of King Lear Author by John W. Draper claims that *King Lear* is truly a great tragedy. The difficulties begin in the very first scene. The old story that Shakespeare chose for his plot was admirably calculated to set forth the timely themes of Divine Right and unity of rule in just the way that his patron James I would have approved;1 but its inescapable initial episodes, in which the old King tries to relinquish his divinely appointed place and to subdivide his realm, and also his casting off of Cordelia and of Kent, seem so improbable that some critics, beginning with Mrs. Lennox in 1753, could cut this Gordian Knot only by declaring that, from the very opening scene, Lear was insane, although a crazy hero seriously impairs the ethical values of the tragedy. In short, the character of Lear, if he is to perform convincingly the initial acts on which the plot depends, must have some adequate motivation; and Shakespeare, who again and again in earlier plays added realistic motivation to his sources, even in comedies which do not require such inevitable structure.[72]

---

70 Dan Brayton, *Angling in the Lake of Darkness: Possession, Dispossession, and the Politics of Discovery in "King Lear"* Source: ELH, Summer, 2003, Vol. 70, No. 2 (Summer, 2003), pp. 399-426 Published by: The Johns Hopkins University Press Stable URL: https://www.jstor.org/stable/30029882

71 Brayton, id: 402.

72 John W. Draper, *The Old Age of King Lear* in The Journal of English and Germanic Philology, Oct., 1940, Vol. 39, No. 4 (Oct., 1940), pp. 527-540 Published by: University of Illinois Press Stable URL: https://www.jstor.org/stable/27704688. p.527.

At the beginning Lear is a consummate politician, a strong ruler, who still has his feelings and considers love more important than power. He may not and, indeed, does not understand the true feelings of Goneril and Regan, but, again, this misunderstanding is largely the result of a condition of kingship and of the demands of kingship. Lear is also a father; he is aware of his responsibilities as father. As William B. Bache considers him,

Lear is about a man who is both father and king. Each of the three plays defines man both in private, familial terms and in public, political terms: Lear is old man, father, and king. The office of king makes its particular, obsessive demands, sub- merging the man or the father to the office: ceremony determines action, as Henry V acknowledges to himself in the night before the battle of Agincourt. A king is flattered and lied to, presented with a view that is unreal and artificial: a king comes to live in, and to believe in, a world not consonant with reality; the image that a king projects and that his subjects perceive is a distorted one. As a matter of fact, I don't think that Lear ever fully understands what he is or what is hap- pening to him. [73]

Bache views the old king as an old man - father - king, but with a significant difference in the last two acts. In part the change is essential because what is done to Gloucester is a demonstration of what could have happened to Lear if he had remained behind, not sent to Dover by Gloucester. He also notes the king's bond to his daughter Cordelia as she is off stage from I, 1, to IV, 4, and perhaps as he calls, "the child transfigured into queen, has usurped the place that Kent, the Fool, and Edgar" had with Lear in the tempest in Act III. In other words, to the" reborn old man - father - king is given the now-perfect offspring." From IV, 4, on, Cordelia's only concern is her father: "He that helps him take all my outward worth." From IV, 7, on, Lear's only concern is Cordelia. As she becomes more than a daughter, Lear becomes more than an old man - father - king: they become canonised by love. Her image and her example change him. [74]

An interesting phenomenon is the usage of negation in correlation with Lear, not only Cordelia and the Fool but Kent also expresses his feelings of negation. In his essay entitled *King Lear and Negation* Edward W. Taylor cites Freud who called man such an animal that is able to express negation.

---

73 William B. Bache, *LEAR AS OLD MAN—FATHER—KING* in CLA Journal, September,1975, Vol. 19, No. 1 (September,1975), pp. 1-9 Published by: College Language Association Stable URL: https://www.jstor.org/stable/44325582 p. 2.

74 Bache, id: 8.

Afterwards he analyzes the connection between "no" and "know" and "nothing" forming a core part of the rhetoric of *King Lear.* He reflects upon the king's importance via the words of his daughters which all contain negation in explicit or subdued form:

At first Lear knows neither himself nor his daughters; the evil characters, unrecognized by the King and Gloucester for what they are, compel the good to say "nothing" (Cordelia), to be "nothing" ("Edgar I nothing am"), or "not to be known" (Kent). Lear will come to know himself first as unaccommodated man on the heath, and later as a "very foolish fond old man." Through negation Lear will fumble his way toward anagnorisi ; through no-ing he will move toward the knowing of Gloucester ("I know thee well enough") and of Cordelia and Kent: "Methinks I should know you, and know this man." As un- accommodated man he comes to "recognize" in plain words plainly spoken - words far removed from the kingly magniloquence that marks the opening of the play. This play, everywhere patterned on principles of division that end in nothing, begins almost immediately to distinguish styles of speech as well as styles of conduct. The magniloquence of Lear calls forth the fulsome protestations of Goneril and Regan, diametrically opposed to the "plainness" of Kent and Cordelia. Although Lear on the heath seeks to "out-scorn" the blasts, the winds in their fury "make nothing of" him (3.1.9), and the old king's 2. Standard Edition of the Complete Psychological Works, ed. and trans. James Strachey (24 vols.; London, 1953- 1974), XIX (1961), pp. 235-39. Cf. René A. Spitz, No and Yes: On the Genesis of Human Communication (New York, 1957): the "unconscious does not have a 'No,'" and the prototypical motor responses of head-nodding and head-shaking "arise in the period of non- differentiation, when not only 'Yes' was indistinguishable from 'No', but when crying is confused with laughing by the observer" (146). Maire Jaanus Kurrik, *Literature and Negation* (New York, 1979), provides an extensive bibliography as well as stimulating insights, and Rosalie Colie, *Paradoxia Epidemica* (Princeton, 1966), has drawn attention to what amounts to an obsession with "nothing" during the Renaissance; on Lear see esp. pp. 463-81. 3. Hugh L. Kennedy, *"King Lear: Recognizing the Ending,"* Studies in Philology, 71 (1974), 371-84, for a well-nigh exhaustive account of the huge number of recognitions, mis-recogni- tions, and near-recognitions. Cf. W. F. Blissett, *"Recognition in King Lear,"* in Some Facets of "King Lear", ed. Rosalie L. Colie and F. T. Flahiff (Toronto, 1974), pp. 103-16. elemental declamations begin to give way to moments of rhetorical plainness, as his grandiloquent manipulation of the royal "we" de- scends into first-person humility or veers into the "we" of our com- mon humanity; he divests himself of his royal robes and of what Renaissance rhetoricians called the "clothing" or "garment" of style. No longer does he speak grandly of "wide-skirted meads" (1.1.64) but moves from the imperative "Come; unbutton here" (3.4.107) to that final entreaty: "Pray you, undo this button" (5.3.308); he has cast off the lendings of language.[75]

Taylor says Lear does not know himself nor his daughters at the beginning, this not knowing nothing criteria is applicable to him in the course of the play, he is going to get to know the truth, and by doing so he is going to get to know himself, recognize the folly and be able to adore Cordelia again, whose nothing was the truth itself. The absurdity of Lear's nothing that is not expressed but felt, will transform to Cordelia's explicit nothing with the aid of the Fool whose sentence marks an important stage in Lear's personal enlightenment: "Nothing will come out of nothing." Lear thus seems to become an absurd symbol, the king of nothing and that of not knowing, with a childish belief in what seems to be glorious and beloved instead of the sheer truth. Justice also fails in this world, natural justice kills Cordelia and thus the king will also die in despair.

Cordelia

Cordelia although a character, she is a symbol herself, mostly recognized as the heart of King Lear. For an ample understanding we shall consider the following two excerpts:

Cordelia's description takes its power from its resonances with other myths, stories, and rituals of death usually followed by resurrection: Christ crowned with thorns; the Green Man or "wild man," whose yearly sacrifice ensures the fertility of the land and its people; and the Biblical Job. But for Shakespeare and his first audiences, this power would have been amplified and inflected by knowledge of the characteristics and properties of the "idle weeds" so carefully and deliberately itemised by Cordelia, and because this image of a neglected harvest fulfils the prophecy of "dearth" made by Edmund in scene 2 of the play.[76]

Judy Kronenfeld puts it in another way, she calls our attention to the triangle of the three girls, placing them to opposing poles:

---

75 Edward W. Taylor, *King Lear and Negation* in English Literary Renaissance, Vol. 20, No. 1 (WINTER 1990), pp. 17-39 Published by: The University of Chicago Press Stable URL: https://www.jstor.org/stable/43447291 Accessed: 27-04-2021 10:00 UTC p. 18-19.

76 Jayne Elisabeth Archer, Richard Marggraf Turley and Howard Thomas, *The Autumn King: Remembering the Land in "King Lear"* Shakespeare Quarterly, Winter 2012, Vol. 63, No. 4 (Winter 2012), pp. 518-543 Published by: Oxford University Press Stable URL: https://www.jstor.org/stable/41819767

France's description of her emphasises her unprotected nakedness in contrast to the grace of parental favour she formerly enjoyed—in accordance with the biblical use of clothing and nakedness to figure protective love and destitution, respectively. However, by using the words as she exits, Cordelia obliquely and more positively associates herself with the naked truth that is the daughter of time, and associates her sisters with the corruption and menace hidden behind voluminous or many-folded garments such as are worn by the Whore of Babylon, or the bedecked harlot exemplifying the false church. [...] the idea of "naked truth" is not exclusive property of Prtotestant or Catholic, Puritan or Anglican. Both Mary Tudor and Elizabeth thus use the motto" Veritas filia Temporis", truth the daughter of Time...[77]

As she appears previously, the daughter of time, she is seemingly unprotected but her will keeps her fighting for her liberty then for her father. She is a protestor, a woman of faith, can one consider her a Protestant amongst the Catholics, someone who refuses to pretend love for inheritance. Cordelia is often interpreted as the sibling of the Fool, where she disappears, he appears, and the truth they say is also very much alike. As for the quarto and folio distinction in this respect hereby we quote Thomas B. Stroup:

The suggestion of the doubling of the two parts arose as a means for explaining the disappearance of the Fool in Act III, as well, indeed, as for his failure to appear or even be mentioned in the first scene of the play. Miss Janet Spens thinks the parts were doubled because Cordelia and the Fool never appear on the stage at the same time, because the two roles call for the same kind of voices, and because there seems to have been a boy actor (some have suggested Armin) with a voice proper to the singing of the whimsical songs required by such roles as Ophelia, Desdemona, Feste, and the Fool in Lear. Actor aside, these are pertinent facts: Cordelia is banished in the first scene with truth for her dowry; the Fool appears 357 lines later (I. iv. i05); he speaks his last line, saying that he will "go to bed at noon" (III. vi. 9i), a line not in the Quarto, and is urged off the stage by Kent shortly thereafter (III. vi. io7), not to appear again-at least in his proper person. After a full scene of preparation for her return to the stage, and exactly 356 lines after the Fool's final exit, Cordelia makes her re- entry. Between Cordelia's exit and the Fool's entry the same number of lines are spoken as between the Fool's final exit and Cordelia's re-entry. Time is exactly meted out for some reason, probably for the change of costume and make-up, if 1 Alois Brandl, Shakespeare (Berlin, i894), p. I79. See also the same book revised as Shakespeare:

77 Judy Kronenfeld, *King Lear and the Naked Truth, Rethinking the Language of Religion and Resistance* (Duke University Press, 1998): 107.

Leben, Umwelt, Kunst (Berlin, I922), pp.369 ff. 2 Among others Brander Matthews, Shakespeare as Playwright (New York, I9I3), pp. i87-i88, suggests that Wilson doubled as the Fool and Cordelia. Alwin Thaler, Shakespeare's Silences (Cambridge, Mass., I929), p. 38, thinks it a plausible theory; whereas W. J. Lawrence, Pre-Restoration Stage Studies (Cambridge, Mass., I927), pp. 72-73, thinks it unlikely on the ground that doubling was not customary for extensive roles. The editor of The Tragedy of King Lear (Yale Shakespeare, New Edition, revised by Tucker Brooke, I9I7), p. I73, n., thinks that probably Armin took the two parts. Miss Janet Spens, Elizabethan Drama (London, i922), p. 25, thinks the theory sound. Arthur J. Stringer, "Was Cordelia the King's Fool?" The Shakespeare Magazine, III (Jan., i897), i-II. Disregarding the text, he argues that Cordelia disguises herself as the Fool and, like Edgar, cleaves to her foolish father. 4 Since Q2, 1619, was a reprint of Ql, 16o8, I follow custom in referring to the two merely as "Quarto". we can trust our reconstruction of the text of the play from the Quarto. The preciseness of this measuring has seemingly gone unnoticed hitherto.It may argue for the accuracy of the text.[78]

An additional sound element is Cordelia's disguise that remembers that of the Fool's introduced by Thomas Stroup. Cordelia pretends that she does not love her father more than natural bond requires. The text of the Quarto and the Folio sound as follows:

The History of King Lear says: "What shall Cordelia do? Love and be silent."[79]

Whereas the same is a bit altered in the Tragedy of King Lear: "What shall Cordelia speak? Love and be silent."[80]

The difference between "do" and "speak", so activity and logos is to be marginally analysed by using Geza Kallay's assertion presented in his dissertation on Othello.

To understand ambiguities, which is also the property of Shakespearean drama, it is essential to examine language. The ethical examination of language, taking into account the interpretations of Géza Kállay's Shakespeare, must begin with an ethical examination of the *logos*, which first came to the center of rhetorical practice in public life, politics and legal procedures in ancient

---

78 Thomas B. Stroup, *Cordelia and the Fool* in Shakespeare Quarterly, Spring, 1961, Vol. 12, No. 2 (Spring, 1961), pp. 127-132 Published by: Oxford University Press Stable URL: https://www.jstor.org/stable/2867387: p. 127-128.

79 Cordelia qtd in The History of King Lear, 1.1.584 The Northon Shakespeare. Q version

80 Cordelia qtd in The Tragedy of King Lear, 1.1.585 The Northon Shakespeare. F version.

Greece and Rome. An ethical examination of the *logos* in absurd interpretations is inevitable, as it is always present as a deficiency and is not given sufficient prominence. "The logos is built around truth, signifying the speech that "directs the soul." It is a technique, which manipulates rhetoric with its persuasive, language actions, also included the dishonest means of persuasive appearance. In Aristotle, the character of the orator already appears, also as an important aspect, but the truth (aletheia) is replaced by the probable (to eikos)."[81]

The persuasive language of the two orators, Goneril and Regan is in opposition with Cordelia's love language. "Your dear highness' love" is the phrase Regan uses for her father in the *History of King Lear*, whereas Cordelia speaks simple and only the truth:

"Then poor Cordelia
And yet not so, since I am sure my love's
More richer than my tongue."[82]

We can note here that there is only a slight difference regarding these sentences in *The Tragedy of King Lear*:

"Then poor Cordelia—
And yet not so, since I am sure my love's
More ponderous than my tongue."[83]

To understand what Cordelia means by nothing and love we may set in parallel her further speech to her father in the two versions:

Good lord,
You have begot me, bred me, loved me.
I return those duties back as are right fit—
Obey you, love you, and most honour you.
Why have my sisters husbands if they say

81 Kállay Géza, *„Nem puszta szó rendít meg így" (IV. 1, 41) Shakespeare Othellója nyelvfilozófiai megközelítésében.* dissertation. available at: 2013. 10.15.

82 Cordelia, The History of King Lear, 1.1.586.

83 Cordelia, The Tragedy of King Lear, id: 1.1.587-

They love you all? Haply when I shall wed
That lord whose hand must take my plight shall carry
Half my love with him, half my care and duty.
Sure, I shall never marry like my sisters,
To love my father all.[84]

The Tragedy of King Lear exposes the following:

Good my lord,
You have begot me, bred me, loved me.
I return those duties back as are right fit—
Obey you, love you, and most honour you.
Why have my sisters husbands if they say
They love you all? Haply when I shall wed
That lord whose hand must take my plight shall carry
Half my love with him, half my care and duty.
Sure, I shall never marry like my sisters.[85]

The two excerpts are very much alike except the fact that in the second version the last sentence is omitted. These words show a deep love and sense of duty towards her father as well as true honour and respect towards the king and what he represents, an icon.

"The children of the tragedies rebelling against their parents will never be fathers or mothers. And this is exemplified not only by the romantic tragedy of *Romeo and Juliet*, but by the great tragedies that mirror human existence, especially King Hamlet and Lear. [...]

Let's face it: although the world operates according to the laws of parents, old men, Shakespeare is almost always on the side of young people and children here too. Whether this world is, say, Denmark and Britain - a "prison" or a "rotten one" and that it is maintained only by the law of hypocrisy, licking, flattery, that is, sin, is only the feeling, the thinking, the truth he appears as a loving and morally sensitive being. Such a "internally controlled " young man with "spiritual eyes" is Hamlet, the Danish prince, and Cordelia, the British princess. They are the people who can see and thus judge, for whom true and false, good and evil, reality and appearance, are divided. They are the celebrants of the »world«, the rejectors of roles and expectations, the renunciators of long-established rites. They are the ones who

84 Cordelia, The History of King Lear, 1.1.586.

85 Cordelia, The Tragedy of King Lear, id. 1.1.587.

are vigilant and careful while the laity, the insensitive and infected people are asleep, perhaps drunk drunk on wine and power, or just madly mad. These seeing children are fools according to the values of the world, because their wisdom is from elsewhere [...]: from above. "[86]

They are the ones who are always out of line, paying dearly for their outbreak attempt, recognizing their beneficial effects on their environment mostly post mortem, but without them there would be no development or social progress.

This category includes Cordelia, who fights against the "false world," the "law of sin," defined in Ophelia's madness, which also maintains a state wasted for crumbs of love, "wounded" by the absurdity of Lear's decision, "plagued by hard times". (Rec. 5, Scene. 3, p. 560)

Shakespeare further develops the spiritual beauty of Ophelia in the figure of Cordelia, endowing her with an already acting force that allows classical values to survive and be rescued from the chaos of an all-encompassing, absurd world. This "seeing child" does not even have "eyes" and "tongues" against his father to understand the parent's action against the child. In 1.1. Cordelia says:

I yet beseech your majesty,
If for I want that glib and oily art
To speak and purpose not—since what I well intend
I'll do't before I speak—that you make known
It is no vicious blot, murder, or foulness,
No unchaste action or dishonoured step
That hath deprived me of your grace and favour,
But even the want of that for which I am richer—
A still-soliciting eye, and such a tongue
That I am glad I have not, though not to have it
Hath lost me in your liking.[87]

Her eyes do not see the appearance but the depths of the human soul. She knows that her sisters are merely pretending love, but they are actually evil and deceitful.

---

86 Fabiny Tibor, Megvakult szülők – látó gyermekek http://www.csipetnyiso.hu/169.cikk.megvakult_szulok_lato_gyermekek

87 Cordelia, The Tragedy of King Lear, 1.1.593.

"I know you what you are,/ and like a sister am most loath to call/ Your faults as they are named." (1.1.594. *The History of King Lear*). She testifies to a high degree of wisdom considering her young age when she foretells, "Time shall unfold what pleated cunning hides." (1.1.594. The *History of King Lear.)*

Honest, open, she takes all the insidiousness, she just says what she thinks is true, even if it makes her denied and exiled.

According to our interpretation, Cordelia is the only classical character of the four heroines of the "four great tragedy" (A.C.Bradley) to keep her *Dasein* all the time, a true forward-thinking reformer princess. She is not enveloped in an ontology, she herself is the miracle of the ontology, the alpha and omega of existence, the purest female character in the Shakespeare canon, who rises above the other female figures in her struggles and holdings.

Heidegger, dissecting *Dasein*, in his analysis of *Being and Time* (1927), dissecting the actually conscious consciousness of existence and oneness, highlights the ontic priority that provides an opportunity to rethink Shakespeare's interpretations. After the English translation of Joan Stambaugh Heidegger, he wrote the *Introduction*, in which he states the starting point of his philosophy:

Both being and time are concepts which have a long history in the metaphysical tradition going back to Plato. In fact, Heidegger uses these two concepts to establish what metaphysics is in his conception of it: Metaphysics begins when Plato separates the realm of Being (the Forms of Ideas) and the realm of time (becoming existence). Thus, Heidegger must take these two terms which define his conception of metaphysics and attempt to give them a non-metaphysical thinking.[Joan Stambough, Martin Heidegger: On Time and Being. Introduction, IX][88]

Moving along the line of conscious being-consciousness, in the first scene of the first act of the play (p. 458) examining Lear's daughters 'love on a pharmacy scale, we are following Stanley Cavell's claim (*Disowning Knowledge. The Avoidance of Love in Six Plays of Shakespeare*). According to Cordelia, she experiences her decision as her own personal responsibility.

First, she chooses conscious listening, she doesn't want to lie like her sisters because it would mean disregarding herself, giving up her moral stance. Then, as a reformer princess, she emerges

88 Joan Stambaugh, Martin Heidegger: On Time and Being. Introduction, IX. www.google.com. »at 11.12. 2015.

from behind the shield of silence and begins to speak, taking on the pitfalls of the logos and openly confronting social malice. Cordelia's character portrayal emerges in post-Cavell, and thus in today's and tomorrow's discourse, as in a pre-Heidegger literary trend, but this work does not follow either of them.

Careful selection of her words to surround the father and king with due respect suggests that we are confronted with an already mature, mature woman who knows exactly what words to use and how. Thus, at the frontier of mature femininity, she becomes a true classic princess who also survives the explanation of Jan Kott as Michael Holahan puts it:

I find Cordelia's value located in her soft voice and "ripe lip" (4.3.20), and I wish to link these descriptions to Lear's final summons to our close attention: "Look on her, look, her lips" (5.3.309). This essay raises issues of stability of character, considering changes in the dying Edmund as preliminary to changes that occur for Lear. In my argument Lear changes by looking for and imitating Cordelia's soft voice; his character change is not solely a development of internal depth but is also an acquired responsiveness to another character. Character evolves not as a formation around a void but as a progressive delineation of spaces between or beyond distinct figures onstage. Instability in this case is no hindrance to character as meaning; it is a groundwork for varied effects of meaning. My goal is to emphasise this interpretation but also to keep in view a theoretical proposition concerning subjectivity.[89]

Cordelia is a symbol of fidelity and love, in the spirit of always telling the truth. Her figure suggests that through her Shakespeare wanted to portray the liberation of the female mindset, which she already endowed with acting power. Cordelia's role echoes that of a fool: both tell the truth. They could even swap places.

Telling the truth is permissible to the fool, but it makes the non-fool a fool in the eyes of society. His path is the society-designated path of the *das man* of Heidegger, in the dust of which he encounters natural elements living with absurd influences that also threaten Lear; they tease his individuality, test Heidegger's oneness, but fail to destroy his classical treasures.

---

89 Michael Holahan, *"Look, Her Lips": Softness of Voice, Construction of Character in King Lear* Source: Shakespeare Quarterly, Winter, 1997, Vol. 48, No. 4 (Winter, 1997), pp. 406-431 Published by: Oxford University Press Stable URL: https://www.jstor.org/stable/2871252. p.407.

In the shadow of Stanley Cavell and Northrop Frye, we continue to look for the absurd features that fill the ontic space that Cordelia enters after being "expelled" from the palace. There can be no real happiness in this ontic space. Even King France cannot make up for the feeling of lack created by the breaking of her soul. Cordelia stands alone in her ontic space, fighting between two knives for her faith. One knife is the pseudo-sisterly love of Regan and Goneril, the other is a storm of natural elements that have become absurd, symbolically delaying the classic essence of his character but still failing to deprive him of his treasures.

Allegorical denigration is taking place in King Lear. Lear wants to castrate the Evil in the transcendent with the power of Regan and the black magic inherent in Goneril (who deprives Gloucester of his most precious organ, his eyes), and she also seeks to deprive Cordelia of her significance. However, Cordelia decides to fight: she struggles with the absurd for the classic treasures:

Oh my dear father, restoration hang
Thy medicine on my lips, and let this kiss
Repair those violent harms that my two sisters
Have in thy reverence made![90]

The alienation of which Cordelia becomes a part by telling the truth inevitably entails the absurd. For her moral spine, she is excluded from the circle that meant the safety of the family. Thus, there is a break in her life and Cordelia has no choice but to leave the palace world. Among her claimants, the prince of Burgundy, who longs for wealth, turns away from her, but she herself refuses him, but accepts King France, whose spiritual treasures are more important than worldly ones.

The discarded, denied girl still asks her sisters to take care of their father. Her noble heart is also shown by the fact that he does not act out of self-interest, but out of concern: she sees her father's blindness, but she cannot help him. Not anymore. Custom does not allow. The girl must bow her head against her father's will, and calm down in her new position. She goes away.

The fool is the one who is about the king's living conscience, answering Lear's poetic questions. Lear is no longer himself when he talks to Goneril. Lear begins to realise that what his fool is saying may be true.

---

90 Cordelia. 4.6.710. both versions alike

Cordelia says in the French camp,
Oh kind gods,
Cure this great breach in his abused nature,
The untuned and hurrying senses O wind up
Of this child-changed father![91]

A father who has become a child assumes a child, who has become a mother. Cordelia acts like she were Lear's mother. The missing mother figure returns in the character of the youngest girl. Lear doesn't even make a reference to his mother or wife, so we can assume they died long before the drama began. Cordelia is the only one who, with her care, fills the role of the missing woman and mother who, out of a sense of childhood duty, stands beside her father when she has gone through hell spiritually.

Julia Kristeva's interpretation of the narrative can also open up exciting space for drama interpretation, and can be used specifically to decipher Cordelia's character. According to Kristeva, the dual instinct (positive / negative, life instinct / death instinct) characteristic of narrative articulates in the form of a kind of non-separation. This non-separation also serves a more accurate understanding of psychology, the denial of the gender difference, and perhaps Shakespeare's characterization. Kristeva argues that social organisation must be under the dominance and control of the family structure. "If this structure breaks down, so does the narrative structure. The prism through which instincts penetrate the family structure, actually stretching the framework of the narrative, is the prism of life."[92]

We can use all this for drama interpretation: the prism of life stretches the framework of the drama, makes it absurd, as the family structure becomes absurd: the ungrateful children become the leaders, the leading parent becomes the annihilated, orphaned child until the third girl finds it.

Cordelia, whose "word was gentle, gentle and quiet," is a multiple victim. First, she was a victim of her father, unable and unwilling to meet her father's absurd expectations, so she became denied, then a victim of Goneril and Edmund, against whom she did nothing but evil could destroy for no reason. Although Cordelia was associated with the absurdity in which Lear suffered from squeezed and reversed

91 Cordelia. *The History of King Lear.* 4.6.710.
92

family roles, she was able to maintain her nobility, keeping herself, and the simplicity and transparency of her thoughts throughout.

In a world set on top of his head, however, she is inevitably lost because, although resembling the character of a fool, she lacks the absurd humour, dialectic, and paradox of the fool's astringent. "The language of the Fool is the language of the grotesque stage of today." Cordelia's language, on the other hand, enlivens the Renaissance. Lear's realisation that Cordelia and the Fool loved him truly and represented the truth in the same way is too late: Cordelia is the victim of the absurd.

Northrop Frye places special emphasis on the interpretation of three words in relation to King Lear. The role of Cordelia in the drama is very interesting and even understandable if we discuss it in the light of Frye's assertions. Frye's keywords for this tragedy are "nature," "nothing," "fool," meaning "nature," "nothing," "fool."[93]

He looked for these three words in Shakespeare's play and interpreted their significance. Shakespeare attached his piece to these three words, and if we think about it more closely, their frequent occurrence is not accidental, since there is also a logical connection among them. If nature turns itself in a foolish mode, or in a foolish world where all the lakes stand, all values and conventional bonds, then the direct consequence is absurd or nothing. This is just my own reverberation for Frye's highly educated, beautifully crafted argument, the essence of which can be summarised as follows: nature is interpreted differently by Lear, Edmund, and Goneril. For, according to the original, contemporary conception, the sphere above nature is the heavenly, above which heaven is situated, the abode of God. It goes back to the expulsion of Adam and Eve, which resulted in the appearance of "fallen physical nature," that is, the fall of physical nature, of human nature, which pushed man deep into the demonic world, while nature, in its noble simplicity, also, it belonged to the higher regions of the noble and the beautiful. When Edmund speaks of nature, he may also think of the fall of human nature, in any case associating this word with the demonic world, and not with the divine, that is, with original nature, we might say: with the natural, but on the contrary, he makes the unnatural natural. Goneril shares this worldview as she also acts in the power of the underworld forces.

Even if she fails, the beauty of the struggle remains. Frye discusses the different scenes of the natural treasures of the natural elements and terrestrial spheres and makes Goneril the main bearer of negative

93 Northrop Frye, On Shakespeare, New Haven and London: Yale University Press, 1986, 105–106.

symbolism with the sentence that he is cursed for treating his father as not a "natural" treatment, not exhausts the connotations of the natural marker.

What could Frye mean by that? Probably he tried to reveal and contrast the distorted logic of the deceitful father-son, father-daughter relationship in Edmund and Goneril before us with the true love and childlike purity symbolized by Cordelia.

In *Shakespeare's Our Contemporary, King Lear, or Endgame*, after comparing it to the heights of Dante, Kott turns the tragedy of the old King written by Shakespeare into a black stage play or "black theatre" of romance. He then continues: "The theme of *King Lear* is the decay and fall of the world. [...] Between the prologue and the epilogue there is a civil war."[94]

In such a world, Cordelia has the right to choose to listen as a shield for her uniqueness and struggle for existence. Can she remain between two knives, though she can symbolically elevate her classical treasures to the ranks of the absurd on a royal rank, can she reform and forge her father's shattered identity again?

Cordelia hopes for renewal, truth, life, but as the drama begins to live with absurd elements, the absurd in the ordinary sense (aimless eye-kicking, royal madness, moral blindness, a foolish rattlesnake-free king) she must die, for truth is the only one that cannot become absurd. At least not with Shakespeare.

Kent

Ronald W. Cooley in his essay entitled *Kent and Primogeniture in "King Lear"* asks the question: Why is Shakespeare's Kent called Kent? His answer is explicit showing the symbolic connotations:

It is a little surprising that the question has been so seldom asked, given that King Lear's only precisely named location is in Kent: Dover, where both Lear and Gloucester flee to meet Cordelia and her French army. Names, however arbitrary and conventional, almost invariably evoke specific associations, particularly when they are also aristocratic titles (Kent is, after all, the Earl of Kent), laden with associations linked to the towns, counties, and regions from which those titles are derived. Ronald W. Cooley is Professor of English at the University of Saskatchewan. His current work on early

94 Jan Kott, *King Lear or Endgame* in *Shakespeare Our Contemprary* (USA: Anchor Books, 1966): 152.

modern *Tunbridge Wells* is part of a larger program of research on the literary and cultural history of Kent. Kent and King Lear the names of all King Lear's male principals are "hieroglyphs of value, from which an entire system can be reconstructed." Beyond linking Kent to the portion of Lear's legacy that would have been Cordelia's, however, Berry does little to identify the specific values his name might conjure up, or to work out the implications of those values for the play as a whole. We can begin to reconstruct those values by considering William Wordsworth's 1803 sonnet invoking the stereotype of the proud and rugged "Men of Kent" as the "Vanguard of Liberty," a stereotype that was already well established in Shakespeare's day. It is a stereotype that seems, at first glance, entirely consistent with the character Shakespeare creates, the volatile yet supremely loyal counsellor, who insists that it is his duty to be "unmannerly / When Lear is mad."But Wordsworth, arriving late on the scene, and writing in a highly compressed form, tells only part of the story. When Wordsworth refers to "the charters that were [theirs] before," he is referring to "gavelkind," Kent's distinctive system of land tenure, which dictated partible inheritance, rather than the prevailing English system of primogeniture. This detail is especially interesting in the context of Shakespeare's King Lear. (...) Through the figure of Kent, Shakespeare evokes the distinctive Kentish character celebrated in Wordsworth's sonnet, and in Shakespeare's day, in works such as William Lambardes' *Perambulation of Kent* (1576).[95]

He explains that when Kent upbraids the king for his folly in dividing his estate, he seems to repudiate the inheritance practises for which his county was famous, "the charters that were [theirs] before," which the men of Kent had preserved from Norman influence. Thus, Shakespeare's Kent is at once the epitome and the antithesis of the stereotypical "man of Kent."

As Michael Warren points out, Kent is "associated with Cordelia as a spokesman for truth, fearless in his honesty and rashly brave." This characterization is evident in the early scenes of both the Folio and Quarto versions of Shakespeare's play. We shall note also that he, like Perillus, remains a faithful servant to his master after the king's dispossession. However, in the Folio version of the play, Shakespeare makes a series of calculated alterations in the role, changes that focus attention on dynastic issues, and thus indirectly accentuate Kentish associations. Beyond the name change, Shakespeare alters the thrust of Perillus/Kent's critique of the king's action.[96]

---

95 Ronald W. Cooley, *Kent and Primogeniture in "King Lear"* in Studies in English Literature, 1500-1900, Spring, 2008, Vol. 48, No. 2, Tudor and Stuart Drama (Spring, 2008), pp. 327-348 Published by: Rice University Stable URL: https://www.jstor.org/stable/40071337 pp. 327-328.

96 Cooley, id: 330.

Being an advocate for Cordella, his defence of the young princess becomes a sign of political objection, in multiple senses, when "state" seems to imply both Lear's royal dignity and the body part. Kent's name and the plot of King Lear are linked to the archetypal character of the "Men of Kent," to the popular reputation of the county. In a discussion, Terry Reilly draws on local detail to explore "the interplay of dramatic form and contemporary legal discourse" in the play. According to Reilly, "[b]oth the County and the Earl of Kent . . . provide for the 'mingling' of . . . oppositional features, thus serving as the chiastic nexus of both the plots and the characterizations." Richard Halpern relies on William Harrison's disapproving account of Kentish gavelkind in his 1587 *Description of England*, in order to suggest that "[t]he name of Shakespeare's Kent . . . may well have been intended to evoke the one county in England where the practice of gavelkind continued.[97]

As the particular Kentish virtues are braveness and diligence, honesty (prosperity, courage, and independence of spirit arise from the landholding and inheritance practises of the county: "in place of . . . the custom of Gavelkind, prevailing everywhere, in manner every man is a freeholder, and hath some part of his own to live upon)[98] It is not by chance that Shakespeare chose this name for the character who serves the king truly, even when he is mad and raging against him. Thus, he becomes the eyes of the king symbolically, whereas Cordelia his heart.

Cooley even exploits the original political aspect of the county of Kent, supposing it has a sound impact on Shakespeare's choice:

Yet if Kent's independent spirit links him to the Kentish yeomanry and peasantry, his dynastic priorities identify him with Kent and King Lear the Kentish aristocracy. In spite of Lambarde's lofty testimonials to gavelkind and its shaping influence on the spirit of the men of Kent, Kentish landowners were, by the sixteenth century, increasingly embracing the dynastic logic of primogeniture, and seeking legal means to leave their estates intact to their eldest sons. But since gavelkind had the force of law in Kent, it could only be extinguished by statute. Hence, in the sixteenth century, "dozens of Kent gentry joined in promoting private acts of parliament to formally exempt their lands from the common custom of the county." According to local historian C. W. Chalklin, "by the seventeenth century, primogeniture had displaced the custom of gavelkind among the Kentish gentry: most or all the land passed to the

97 Cooley, id: 331.

98 Lambardes, *Perambulation of Kent* qtd. In Cooley, id: 332.

elder son, thus establishing his superior social and economic standing. "The county of Kent, then, was already ideologically divided on inheritance matters by Shakespeare's time.[99]

As Cooley calls it, *King Lear* is the play of affection and bonds, parental bonds, it suggests that it was a vision toward which Shakespeare would have inclined in the context of an emerging early modern debate about primogeniture. The playwright's concern with matters of dynasty and property has to come into focus. Inheritance is also an additional core element of the plot of the play.

Edgar's "sullen" humor

The title page of the first Quarto edition in *King Lear* contains the following: "His True Chronicle Historie of the Life and Death of King Lear and his three Daughters. With the unfortunate life of Edgar, sonne and heire to the Earle of Gloster, and his sullen and assumed humour of Tom of Bedlam… ""Sullen" in Shakespeare has the strong meaning of melancholia or depression, a variety of madness assumed by Edgar in his disguise as Tom of Bedlam. Harold Bloom asks: "Why does Edgar assume the lowest possible disguise?" His answer is as follows:

There is something so profoundly disproportionate in Edgar's self-abnegation throughout the play that we have to presume in him a recalcitrance akin to Cordelia's, but far in excess of hers. (…) The recognition encounter, which kills Gloucester, is one of Shakespeare's great unwritten scenes, being confined as it is to Edgar's narrative account, delivered to Albany after Edmund has received his death wound. (…) If we speak of a poetic rather than dramatic centre to the tragedy, we might choose the meeting between the mad King Lear and the blind Gloucester in Act 4 Sc6, l: 80-185.[100]

The symbol of charity, Edgar as Poor Tom, guides his father. This seems to be the highest "emotional topic in the drama, the theme of charity in human relations: the desperate need which human beings have for each other, and their paradoxical inability to satisfy that need," --as Sears Jayne characterises this piece.[101]

---

99 Cooley, id: 334.

100 Harold Bloom, *King Lear* in The Invention of the Human (New York: Riverhead Books, 1998): 480-481.

101 Sears Jayne, *Charity in King* in Lear Shakespeare Quarterly, Spring, 1964, Vol. 15, No. 2 (Spring, 1964), pp. 277-288 Published by: Oxford University Press Stable URL: https://www.jstor.org/stable/2867900 p. 277.

It is Richard C. McCoy, who pins Edgar's recognition to analysis, reminding us the Christian emblems of the play mentioned at the beginning of the chapter:

In King Lear, recognition of Edgar "as a real person and a real son" is complicated by Edgar's own relentless moralising. Edgar is an exemplary but problematic figure. As Janet Adelman says, the "absolute goodness and nobility of Edgar . . . has been assumed in much of the criticism of the twentieth century . . . at the price of overlooking certain questions raised by his behaviour." Edgar's predilection for smug sententiousness constitutes one of his most questionable characteristics. Maynard Mack sees him as a Morality figure whose pronouncements provide "the 'meaning' before we are given the event," and Mack treats Lear as a tragedy "that is as much homiletic as it is dramatic, and sometimes more the former than the latter."Edgar's aphorisms about the uses of adversity and the comforts of compassion can be edifying, and his own experience confirms that, in suffering, "the mind much sufferance doth o'erskip, / When grief hath mates, and bearing fellowship" (3.6.104–5). At the same time, his maxims are often frequently disrupted and denied by the play's escalating sequence of shocks and horrors, and the dramatic undercuts homiletic assurances. Confident that his suffering may prove a redemptive blessing in disguise, he asserts that "The lamentable change is from the best; / The worst returns to laughter."[102]

All these lead us to the conclusion that Edgar seems to be a morality figure, just like in the old morality plays, whose main significance lies in telling the truth, questioning the hardness in life, punishing himself for his deficiencies, yet uplifting the mood of his father, being a good loyal son, not letting him despair in pain over the loss of his son and that of his eyesight. Edgar's linguistic elements vary from the Fool's vocabulary to the philosophical dimensions, the orator here is an individual taking responsibilities in life, caring for the old Gloucester, showing emotions.

The last act brings the death of his father and the defeat of Lear, but Edgar is unbowed. Putting aside the rags of Poor Tom, he marches forth in the armour of a knight whose "name is lost" (5.3.120) to challenge his wicked stepbrother to formal combat. In this new guise, he appears as the chivalric embodiment of heroic virtue, resembling those celestial forces invoked by Albany who fears chaos if "the heavens do not their visible spirits / Send quickly down to tame these vilde offences" (4.2.46–47). In this encounter, virtue proves initially victorious, winning the battle but not the war. We soon realise, along with the characters, that the stirring heroics of this scene have distracted us from the mortal plight of Lear and Cordelia. The

102 Richard C. McCoy, *"Look upon me, Sir": Relationships in King Lear* in Representations, Vol. 81, No. 1 (Winter 2003), pp. 46-60 Published by: University of California Press Stable URL: https://www.jstor.org/stable/10.1525/rep.2003.81.1.46 p. 47.

horrific shock caused by that "Great thing of us forgot!" (5.3.235) ultimately shatters all hope of triumph, but not before the pleasures of moralising complacency are given free play. After defeating his villainous brother, Edgar magnanimously proposes to "exchange charity" (5.3.165) and discloses his identity. His account of their father's blinding is remarkably harsh, combining smug sanctimony with misogynistic insult to his brother's bastard origins: "The Gods are just, and of our pleasant vices Make instruments to plague us; The dark and vicious place where thee he got Cost him his eyes. (5.3.169–71)"[103]

The heroic virtue embodied in Edgar at the end however seems to be undermined by the fact that he delays in revealing himself, thus causing suffering to his father who believes Edgar had been lost. Stanley Cavell sees the loss of eyesight as metaphor and consequence of Edgar's behaviour: "Edgar's avoidance of Gloucester's recognition precisely deprives Gloucester of his eyes again."[104]

Centaurs

Shakespeare frequently uses animal images in his play texts to symbolically describe certain humans and their characters. The number of such metamorphic references is outstandingly high in King Lear. To grasp the meaning of such metamorphoses did not present an unsurpassable obstacle for contemporary audiences. They were familiar with, were in everyday contact and lived in the vicinity of animals. After the theatre-goer left his horse in the care of a groom near the theatre, it was not hard to obey the Chorus when they say in Henry the V.'s Prologue: "Think when we talk of horses, that you see them". But the imagination of Shakespearean audiences could take in more than that, since early modern plays featured other 'beasts' as well, like horses or horse-like creatures belonging to different cultural discourses. Most probably nobody was shocked in the audience when King Lear, speaking about his daughters (and probably of all women), howled on the stage:

"Down from the waist they are centaurs,
though women all above. But to the girdle do the
gods inherit; beneath is all the fiend's. There's hell,
there's darkness, there is the sulphurous pit; burning,
scalding, stench, consumption! Fie, fie, fie, pah,
pah!" (Act 4, Scene 6, 140-45)[105]

103 Richard C. McCoy, id: 48.

104 Stanley Cavell, qtd in C. McCoy id: 49.

105 Folger Shakespeare. The History of King Lear.

For the educated the myth where the centaur symbol originated was familiar, and for the uneducated at least the message of it. This myth was the Ixion myth.

In Greek mythology Ixion is the son of Phlegyas, king of the Lapiths. He could not provide his father-in-law with the promised dower and when he cures his son-in-law's horses as guarantee for his claim, Ixion, pretending friendship, summons him and casts him into a pitch of fire. He goes insane about his dreadful deed, but Zeus lifts him from his sin and, being his favourite, also invites him to the banquet of the gods. Here he falls in love with Hera (Juno). Zeus (Jove), to please Ixion, transforms a cloud into the shape of Hera (Juno) and Ixion pairs with the cloud-woman and the centaurs are born. When Ixion boasts with Juno's assumed favour, Zeus casts him into the Tartaros.[106]

In his book on emblems, George Wither highlights how this halfe-a man, and half-a horse (...) ancient Hieroglyphicke teaches the reader/spectator that "Wisdome should be joyne'd with outward force, / If prosperous, we desire our works to be", and finally prays to God to help him in achieving this. He clearly explains what refers to what: "His Upper-part, the shape of Man, doth beare, / To teach, that, Reason must become our guide (...) The hinder-parts, a Horses Members are; / To shew, that we must, also, strength provide."[107] This interpretation of the centaur was the most widespread in Shakespeare's age.

His contemporary, Edward Topsell[108] emphasises the monstrous sexuality surrounding the centaurs. He provides an illuminating contemporary context to Lear's exclamation on unnatural copulation and female centaurs, since Topsell himself seems to revel in the forms of illicit sexuality that surround centaurs – from "buggery" to raping and drunken Centaurs of the Lapiths' banquet. Consequently, based on the concepts highlighted by Topsell's book, Lear's unorthodox reference to female centaurs does not seem such a sudden leap from the traditionally male-centred centaur mythology, since intemperance and illicit sexuality provides an easy link between the two.

An interesting approach is provided by Andreas Höfele[109], who places this tragedy against the background of Europe's celebrated medieval and early modern animal trials, which subjected the

106 *Encyclopedia Révay* (Budapest, 1911).

107 George Wither, *A Collection of Emblemes, Ancient and Moderne*, London, printed by Augustine Matthews, 1635, sig. A2r.

108 Edward Topsell, *The historie of foure-footed beastes*, London, William Jaggard, 1607, p. 319, lines 18-26.

109 In Boehrer, Bruce:. "Andreas Höfele, *Stage, Stake, and Scaffold: Humans and Animals in Shakespeare's Theatre.*" Modern Philology, vol. 111, no. 2, 2013

beast to criminal punishment with various violations of the human legal code. The connection here may be drawn by one of the storm scenes of the play (Quartr Act 3), where Lear fantasized arraignment of his pelican daughters trial parodies actual judicial procedure. Thus, while King Lear "has no hanged pig in human clothes"...it does have the so called 'mocked trial', a trial which works in collusion with the play's opening love test to "measure out and delimit the space of the political". Here and elsewhere Lear not only embodies the "standard judicial practice" of bestializ(ing) the criminal, it also enacts a "bestialization of the representative of law", a reversal of conventional roles, which implies that Lear, too, as a king whose word was law, may have been no more than "a dog's obeyed in office" (Act 4, Scene 6, 173-74).[110]

Hardison[111] emphasises that "Forty-five years after *Gorboduc*[112] has been produced at White Hall for Queen Elisabeth, Shakespeare's *King Lear* was produced before "the Kinges maiestie at Whitehall". It is common of the two dramas that they both work with the motif of division of the kingdom and drew on mythology to articulate their historical materials. It is unnecessary to argue that Shakespeare learned to use the technique from *Gorboduc*. And he used the Ixion's myth. There are two profound proofs of the fact that he must have been thinking of this myth while writing *King Lear* in Act 4: "Thou art a soul in bliss; but I am bound / Upon a wheel of fire (Act 4, Scene 7, 522-54)[113] and when he calls his daughters centaurs in Act 4. The wheel of fire was the punishment of Ixion. The question automatically arises: If the punishment is analogous to those of Ixion, what could the sin be? This question is answered by Lear's calling his daughters centaurs. Most probably Starnes and Stalbert[114] are right saying: "The story of Ixion and his adulterous offspring was in Shakespeare's mind throughout writing the play."

Hardison states that during the Renaissance Ixion and the centaurs were popular figures, familiar to anyone who studied Ovid and Virgil in grammar school. He was one of the four great sinners; Tantalus, Sisyphus and Tytius being the others. Shakespeare never mentions Ixion by name, but refers twice to the centaur already before Lear, both times in connection with the battle of the centaurs (Titus Andronicus, Midsummer Night's Dream). Hardison also provides a cyclorama of the authors

110 Folger Shakespeare. The History of King Lear.

111 Hardison, O. B. *"Myth and History in King Lear."* Shakespeare Quarterly, vol. 26, no. 3, 1975

112 The first English drama.

113 Folger Shakespeare. The History of King Lear.

114 De Witt T. Starnes and Ernest William Talbert: *Classical Myth and Legend in Renaissance Dictionaries* (University of North Carolina Press, 1955).

who discussed the Ixion myth. Myths are in permanent change, no wonder that the approach and interpretation of various authors in various ages somewhat differ.

According to Fulgentius the Ixion myth has two parts: The first is the literary history of Ixion, the ruler, who was "the first Greek to affect prompt rule". As part of this goal he kept one hundred knights who were called centaurs. He was soon overthrown, and his fall is symbolized by a wheel "because the turn of a wheel soon cuts down whatever it holds high".

The attempted seduction of Juno is an allegory. It means that "Who seeks to be more than is proper, will be less than he is." Thus, when Ixion would have seduced Juno, she made a cloud in her shape, and when Ixion coupled with it, he got centaurs.

Bocaccio agrees with Fulgentius that the fable suggests foolish desire for pomp, but he prefers to see Ixion as the first usurper and tyrant rather than as the first vain king. Ixion returned to the earth boasting with his attempted seduction, and was hurdled down to hell by a Jovian thunderbolt. The thunderbolt symbolises the shock of disillusionment that comes when the would-be king realises the difficulty of his situation. The wheel symbolises the ceaseless round of cares that torment him. Ixion is a type of the magistrate who becomes enamoured of the dignitas of office, while neglecting the iustitia. The centaurs have a violent desire for rule, and their battle with the Lapiths is an allegory of the attempt to usurp power.

Comes adds the story of Ixion's murder of his father-in-law Eioneius, for which he wondered the earth unforgiven until Jove had pity on him and raised him to the heaven. Comes offers two important interpretations of the myth. "Those men who seek glory rather than virtue in any affair, or embrace false wisdom rather than the truth, will do many improper things wherefore monster-like centaurs are born from a cloud."

Alexander Ross adds a rather surprising Christian interpretation to the tableau. For him the story of Ixion is a fable of religious ingratitude. It shadows forth the Christian doctrine of man redeemed from original sin. (Ixion's murder, Jove's pardon). And elsewhere: "The centaurs are Ixion's children and symbolise proneness to violet passion, and in particular the passion of lust.

The lady centaur has also tradition: Ben Johnson named an over-sexed lady in Epicoene 'Centaure'; and Alexander Ross insists that "they were said to be halfe horses, imitative of their insatiable lust, and proneness to Venerie".

Hardison concludes that the Ixion myth was conventionally interpreted in two ways: as a political allegory showing the disastrous result of irresponsible rule and as an allegory of ingratitude, both familial and religious. Coupled with them were several corollary motifs such as the idea of providential punishment (Jove's thunderbolt), the idea of lust (the centaurs), emphasis on wealth as a source of power (Juno symbolism), and others.

Motifs of the Ixion Myth in Shakespeare 's *King Lear*

Irresponsibility: The Desire of Dignitas

The earliest and most persistent interpretation of the Ixion myth is that it symbolises the desire for pomp (dignitas) without responsibilities. As Salutati expresses it, "affecting rule, he gets a cloud; that is, he gains the appearance of rule, not its reality". The tragic conclusion of the myth here again teaches the stern moral: "Who strives to be more than is proper, will be less than he is".

Desire for pomp/dignitas without responsibilities is precisely the motif which causes Lear to abdicate in the first scene of King Lear. As soon as the courtiers are assembled, Lear announces,

"...'his is our fast intend
To shake all care and business from our age
Conferring them on younger strength, while we
Unburden 'd crawl toward death. (Act 1, Scene 1, 40-44)[115]

The same is worded in Shakespeare's dramatic source, the Chronicle, as:

"... I would fayne resigne these earthly cares, / and think upon the welfare of my soul".[116] However, Lear is only wearied by his duties. He intends to retain all the trappings of his royal office:

"...Only we shall retain
The name and all th'additions to a king;
The sway, revenue, execution of the rest,
Beloved sons, be yours." Act I, Scenel, 151-54)[117]

115 Folger Shakespeare. The History of King Lear.

116 'Quoted from the reprint of the play in Shakespeare's Library, (London, 1875, vi): 308.

117 Folger Shakespeare. The History of King Lear.

To retain his dignitas, Lear must be surrounded by one hundred knights accountable only to him and must be addressed with the formal title of "king". The resemblance to Ixion's 100 centaurs is striking. When her daughters suggest reducing the number of the knights and Oswald calls him "my lady's father" (Act 1, Scene 4, 89), he flies into an ungovernable rage. But this is not the substance, just the shadows of rule, as the Fool informs Lear that he is: "... Now thou art an 0, without a figure ... thou art nothing." (Act 1, Scene 4, 197-98, 199)[118]

Punishment: The Wheel

The punishment for Ixion's sin is the torture of being bound on a wheel eternally through hell. Lear explicitly compares his experience with that of Ixion when he claims: "...I am bound / Upon a wheel of fire that mine own tears / Do scold like molten lead..." (Act 4, Scene 7, 52-54).[119] This statement is a kind of confession. It is Lear's first admission that he is being punished for some sin. As his senses return he kneels before Cordelia to ask forgiveness. For a moment the wheel ceases to turn, for he has come to terms with what he has made himself: "... Pray you now, forget and forgive; I am old and foolish" (Act 4, Scene 7, 98-99).[120] However, like Ixion, he must suffer further. In the next act the wheel resumes its inexorable motion.

Further significance is added to the wheel image when we recall that Ixion's wheel was interpreted as the wheel of fortune on which man is bound when he allows violent passion to override reason. It is Lear's "hideous rashness" which begins the action of the play, and this rashness recurs in the violent curses of Cordelia, Regan and Goneril. The association of the wheel image in *King Lear* with fortune is made explicit in two references. First, there is Kent's "Fortune, Good-night! Smile once more; turn thy wheel!" (Act 2, Scene 2, 188-189).[121] Second, there is Edmond's dying exclamation: "The wheel is come full circle; I am here" (Act 5, Scene 3, 209).[122]

---

118 Folger Shakespeare. The History of King Lear.

119 Folger Shakespeare. The History of King Lear.

120 Folger Shakespeare. The History of King Lear.

121 Folger Shakespeare. The History of King Lear.

122 Folger Shakespeare. The History of King Lear.

Wealth and Force: The Real Bases of Power

Ixion's disastrous infatuation with the cloud woman was interpreted as an allegorical lesson that authority must be based on the physical realities of money and force. Alexander Ross, commenting on Juno's patronage of money and power, declared that "wealth is everything; it is both meat, drink, cloth, armour, it is that which doth comment on all things" (Mistagogus Poeticus, p. 225).

Lear misinterprets the nature of power in the same way as Ixion. He explicitly gives up "sway", "revenue" and "execution", yet wishes to retain authority. His error is neatly defined by the references to Juno and Jupiter in the scene when he finds Kent in the stocks. He is incredulous, he cannot believe that his authority has been so far flouted. (Juno and Jupiter, Act 2, Scene 4, 23,24).

The importance of wealth is also emphasised by the Fool in several lines:

"Fathers that wear rags
Do make their children blind;
But father that bear bags
Shall see their children kind." (Act 2, Scene 4, 54-58)[123]
And:
"That sir which serves and seeks for gain,
And follows but for form,
Will pack when it begins to rain
And leave thee in the storm." (Act 2, Scene, 4, 84-87)[124]

Authority cannot exist unless it is backed by money and power. As Reagan reminds the hysterical Lear: "I pray you father, being week, seem so" (Act 2, Scene 4, 233).

Lust: The centaurs

Lear's description of his daughters as centaurs is an allusion to the Ixion myth, since the centaurs were the offspring of Ixion, begotten by him on the cloud-woman. Shakespeare associated the offspring of

123 Folger Shakespeare. The History of King Lear.

124 Folger Shakespeare. The History of King Lear.

Lear with the offspring of Ixion. Traditionally the centaurs were considered emblems of masculine lust, "carnal men, made bestial by lust" (*Fulgentius Metaforalis*, IV. 121). Although Shakespeare changes the sex of the centaurs, the emphasis on the idea of lust is preserved.

Natália Prikli[125] investigates deeper into the Ixion myth and its appearance in King Lear. She explains that besides "the elite" centaur of humanist education, the hobby-horse of the morris dance, the wickerwork costume of this dancing, prancing, lascivious and merry character enjoyed outstanding popularity in the decades between 1580 and 1642.

She explains that the first things that were referred to as hobbies were in fact horses, of a breed that was popular in Ireland in the Middle Ages and is now extinct. The Scottish poet, John Barbour, referred to them as 'hobynis', in the narrative poem The Bruce, 1375. In Reliquiae Antiquae, a poetic work of Barbour's from around 1400, he referred to them again, this time with a little more context:

"And one amang, an Iyrysch man,
Uppone his hoby swyftly ran,"

English mummers, morris dance teams and minstrel groups began performing with characters (often children) dressed in wickerwork and cloth costumes, made to look like stylised horses - not altogether unlike the present-day pantomime horses. These 'hobby-horses', which took their name from the Irish breed, are still to be seen as part of the English folk tradition, notably at the annual 'Obby 'Oss festival, celebrated each May Day in Padstow, Cornwall. This custom dates back to at least the 16th century, when a payment for a performance by a hobby-horse was recorded in the Churchwarden's Accounts of St. Mary's Church, Reading, 1557:

"Item, payed to the Mynstrels and the Hobby-horse on May Day, 3s."

As time went by, the name hobby-horse was given to numerous other things; among them to a loose woman or a strumpet. In Shakespeare's *Love's Labour's Lost* for example: "Cal'st thou my love Hobbi-horse?"

The hobby-horse appeared in numerous texts but being the most remembered when it was so famously "forgotten" (in *Hamlet* "For oh, for oh, the hobby-horse is forgot" (Act 3. Scene 2, 144-143).

---

125 Natália Pikli, *Hybrid Creatures in Context: Centaurs, Hobby-horses and Sexualised Women* in Hamlet, King Lear, The Two Noble Kinsmen, (Budapest: Actes des congrès de la Société française Shakespeare, 2020).

The allusions to these half-horse, half-man hybrid creatures frequently intermingled with shrew-taming discourses, which relied on the equation of unruly horses and women. It helps to imagine how the hobby-horse and pertaining gendered popular discourses may have affected the reception and interpretation of such imagery by the contemporary audience. In these Shakespearean passages the elitist centaur mingles with the popular and rural hobby-horse (which was frequently, though not exclusively, associated with the morris dance), which results in a multi-layered representation of the man-horse hybrid. Pikli argues that whereas centaurs could symbolise a mastery of horsemanship in a practical sense, and, by extension, a mastery of reason over passion in allegorical terms (a phenomenon also prominent in emblem books), the playful "dancing-prancing" mastery of the hobby-horse could occasionally discolour the moral message. On the other hand, the monstrosity and bestiality of the hybrid centaur, and especially that of the female centaur in King Lear appears in interaction with the gendered use of the polysemous word 'hobby-horse', which often referred to 'a whore', that is, illicit female sexuality, as in the famous instances in *Love's Labour's Lost, Othello and The Winter's Tale.*

Wither's repercussions of the centaur imagery have been investigated in inspiring studies, with the passage from *King Lear* receiving heightened scholarly attention in informative studies by Laurie Shannon, Eric Brown, Andreas Höfele, Jonathan Bate and others. Pikli's paper goes a step further and claims that the mingling of elite and popular discourses becomes a significant factor in the interpretation of the horse-rider and centaur-like imagery in Claudius's reference to the "French horseman", and in Arcite's death in *The Two Noble Kinsmen*. Lear's famous allusion to his daughters as female centaurs is reconsidered by the author in the light of early modern popular discourses regarding the hobby-horse, which connect illicit sexuality to women and unruly horse-like figures.

The able rider came to symbolise potent rule, reason's mastery over beastly passion, often with a gender bias: contemporary shrew-taming narratives associated unruly horses with unruly women throughout Europe. As Boehrer[126] summarizes, the opposition of the bestial, sexualised female and the rational male was pictured as the horse and rider throughout the early modern world, with the mare frequently becoming "a powerful emblem of feminine unchastity."

Early modern people – as we mentioned above – were in everyday contact with horses and objects which belonged to horsemanship. We have two contemporary pictorial representations of the morris hobby-horse, the so-called Betley Window and Vinckenboom's painting, *The Thames at Richmond,*

126 Bruce Boehrer, *Shakespeare Among the Animals. Nature and Society in the Drama of Early Modern England* (New York, Palgrave/St. Martins Press, 2002).

with the Old Royal Palace. Although they may only be accepted with a pinch of salt regarding authentic representation, due to their synthesising genre requirements, and with the Betley Window synthesised features of different rural festivities from maypole to sword dance, they do attest to the popularity and composite being of the early modern hobby-horse. The stain-glass window in Betley Hall, depicting the month of May, is most probably a mid-sixteenth-century depiction of traditional May Day characters, mostly modelled on Israhel van Meckenem's picture in the late 15th-century Strasbourg Almanac. Significantly, the maypole and the hobby-horse (and some smaller details) are 'Englished' additions to Meckenem's characters, and are without a former continental model. The Window shows this half-man, half-horse hybrid in its full glory, among other festive characters of rural May Games.

Vinckenboom's picture is a landscape painting, and although it seems to give an authentic depiction of a morris dance complete with a hobby-horse, some degree of idealisation, arising from genre expectations, cannot be excluded. The morris hobby-horse in this landscape appears among the morris dancers, without the ladle, since it is now the Fool who interacts with the middle-class and aristocratic onlookers. Nevertheless, these depictions show clearly how this wickerwork costume of the dancing, prancing, flirtatious hobby-horse lived in Shakespeare's contemporaries' imagination.

The most frequent meaning of the word 'hobby-horse' referred to 'loose' women. This gender-switch was partly occasioned by the close association of the morris hobby-horse and unruly women, who often danced and played together during morris dances, in a form of sexual flirtation, to celebrate joyful fertility on such carnivalesque occasions like May Day. This is evident in Cobbes' verses: "But when the Hobby-horse did wihy, / oh pretty wihy, / Then all the Wenches gaue a tihy, / oh pretty tihy." On the other hand, this gender-switch originated in the easy associative leap between unruly women and unruly horses to be tamed and ruled by male reason and power, which was dominant in shrew-taming discourses.

The centaur, on the other hand, is a fully imaginary, and predominantly male being, the word coming to English from Latin and/or French, taking its origins in Greek mythology and Pliny. Therefore, the centaur is strongly connected to elite culture in the early modern imagination, occupying a prominent position in emblem books.

The hybrid nature of the centaur led Physiologus[127] to the idea that the centaur corresponds to the heretic, who is aware of the teachings of Christianity but is unable to employ them in appropriate

127 An ancient Greek book containing stories and tales with moral content about real and mythical animals, Collins English Dictionary, 2014.

ways, therefore his nature remains dual. On the other hand, since Chiron was the wise tutor of Achilles, a beneficent connection to nature and the natural also contributed to the complex imagery of the centaur, together with the idea of wisdom. Based on such disparate trends of tradition, the centaur entered the Renaissance as a highly ambiguous sign. Besides the allusion to the Ovidian duplex natura of the elite centaur, these diverging attributions led to both stigmatisation and adoration of the centaur, ranging from becoming a role model in a Prince's education by Machiavelli to demonization in *King Lear.*

Topsell's huge enterprise deserves some more attention, since it is a compendium of the age's concepts on animals, collecting not only scientific and objective data but completing these with "Narrations out of Scriptures, Fathers, Phylosophers, Physitians, and Poets", as well as with "Hyerogliphics, Emblems, Epigrams, and other good Histories", according to the title page. Relying on his findings Pikli establishes that the mastery of rider above horse is expressed by the imaginative fusing of the two bodies, however, the rider's place on the horse's back differs from the positioning of the upper human part of the centaur, and rather recalls that other famous horse and rider image of the age, the hobby-horse. The image of the popular hobby-horse is superimposed on the elite centaur, especially in the imagination of the less-educated spectators (the groundlings). Shakespeare was careful to cater for the needs of all segments of his audience, therefore, a possible palimpsest of popular and elite associations seems quite plausible.

In the first published volume of his translation of Gesner's magisterial work, Topsell focuses on "four-footed beasts", which may be accounted for the fact that in Shakespeare's contemporaries' imagination, the largest and most visible corpus of animals were quadrupeds, which were called 'beasts'. As Shannon emphasises, the word 'beast' occurs in Shakespeare 141 times as opposed to 'animal', which features only eight times.

And finally about Shakespeare's strong language. When a man calls his daughter 'centaure' it is not gallantry at all. But Lear uses these 'strong' words to express his passion. And he succeeds. Take the mad monarch as he roves the wild heath: "Blow, winds, and crack your cheeks! rage! blow!…Singe my white head!" (Act 3, Scene 2, 1, 7).[128] Or the broken father when he cradles his deceased daughter: "Thou'lt come no more,/ Never, never, never, never, never!" (Act 5, Scene 3, 371-71).[129] The Bard's language plunges us into the depths of Lear's despair.

128 Folger Shakespeare. The History of King Lear.

129 Folger Shakespeare. The History of King Lear.

But King Lear doesn't just feature some of Shakespeare's strongest language. It also showcases some of his, well, strongest language. And when we give it a closer look, much of it is truly below the belt. Recall that King Lear descends into madness as he feels each of his three daughters rejects him. When his eldest, Goneril, objects to some of his post-regnal demands, Lear isn't just indignant: he is downright wrathful and hurls curses. Consider this tirade:

> "Hear, Nature, hear! dear goddess, hear!
> Suspend they purpose, if thou didst intend
> To make this creature fruitful!
> Into her womb convey sterility!
> Dry up in her the organs of increase;
> And from her derogate body never spring
> A babe to honor her! If she must teem,
> Create her child of spleen, that it may live
> And be a thwart, disnatured torment to her!
> Let it stamp wrinkles in her brow of youth;
> With cadent tears fret channels in her cheeks;
> Turn all her mother's pains and benefits
> To laughter and contempt, that she may feel
> How sharper than a serpent's tooth it is
> To have a thankless child! Away, away! (Act 1, Scene 4, 289-303)[130]

Lear's impressions are personal. He curses her as a woman, as a mother. But the curses are also intensely physical, willing her barrenness, deterioration, and suffering. "Strike her young bones,/ You taking airs, with lameness!" (Act 2, Scene 4, 183-184) and the ranging father continues: "Infect her beauty,/ You fen-sucked fogs…!" (Act 2, Scene 4, 187-188). He wishes death and decay for her body. "Thou art a boil,/ A plague-sore, an embossed carbuncle,/ In my corrupted blood" (Act 2, Scene 4, 256-258).[131] He treats his own flesh and blood as a disease.

130 Folger Shakespeare. The History of King Lear.

131 Folger Shakespeare. The History of King Lear.

Lear is revulsed by the female form. It threatens the aged ruler's own waning virility, taunting his own "every inch" as a king (Act 4, Scene 6, 127)[132]. And it's the vagina he most fears and loathes. Yes, for Lear, "hell" is a smelly vagina.

With Lear's vaginal "hell" Shakespeare manages an unholy trinity of profanity, folding taboos of the sacred, sex, and the body all into one. This Elizabethan epithet has antecedents elsewhere in Renaissance literature: Earlier, Boccaccio figures a phallic devil in a hellish vagina in his Decameron, for instance. And pit, ditch, and valley join hell as vulval vulgarities. But what's shocking for the modern reader – and what's consistent with current linguistic trends – are not these traditional taboos of the sacred, sex, and the body. It's his misogyny. It's not any particular curse word, per se, but his curse of a particular group of people: women.

Blindness

The theme of blindness, both literal and metaphoric, is one of King Lear's most prominent themes. This is not surprising in a play, which includes the gouging out – and not behind curtains, but on the open stage – of the Earl of Gloucester's eyes. It is shocking for any audience of any age. There is something about the nature of the eye that makes this awful gouging viscerally upsetting, and also mentally disturbing. The eye is soft, vulnerable, easily hurt. The eye seems to be the primary sense in perceiving the world around us.

Before Cornwall executes this brutal mutilation, Cornwall and Regan repeatedly call their prisoner a "traitor" (Act 3, Scene 7, 4; 9; 25). Goneril says: "Pluck out his eyes" (6), and Regan says: "Hang him instantly" (5).

But such a deed requires a court decision as Cornwall cynically remarks:

> "Though well we may not pass upon his life
> Without the form of justice, yet our power
> Shall do a court'sy to our wrath, which men
> May blame but not control."[133]

132 Folger Shakespeare. The History of King Lear.

133 Cornwall. *The History of King Lear*, id. 3.7. scene 14. p. 674.

Gloucester's punishment would require some sort of trial but Cornwall thinks that no-one will be able to object whatever they do to Gloucester. In this respect he is wrong, because a nameless servant protects and kills him:

1. Servant: "Hold your hand, my lord!
I have served you ever since I was a child;
But better service have I never done you
Than now to bid you hold."[134]

Cornwall acts as a skilled executioner: "Fellows, hold the chair. / Upon these eyes of thine I'll set my foot."[135] And he does. But for Regan it is not enough: "...One side will mock another; the other too."[136] And Cornwall is pleased with the idea: "Lest it see more, prevent it. Out, vile jelly! / Where is thy lustre now?"[137]

The blinding of Gloucester is an example of stage stigma, of using some physical abomination to symbolize the errors and insufficiencies of a character, as Shakespeare did previously with the mutilation of the Andronici - explains Wilson[138] in his relevant essay. As with Shakespeare's other instances of stigma, the blinding of Gloucester poses the question: is it metaphor or metonymy? The actual reason for Gloucester's blinding is that he, alarmed by the mounting tyranny of the Duke of Cornwall, and the rift growing between Cornwall and Albany pledges himself to the French rebellion that will bring Lear back into power, as Gloucester relates to his bastard son, Edmund. With the intent on acquiring his father's fortune, Edmund betrays him to Cornwall, who makes Edmund the new Earl of Gloucester. On the other hand, Gloucester's blinding is probably not only a consequence but also the effect of his mistakes. Edgar voices this view when he says to Edmund: "The dark and vicious place where thee he got cost him his eyes."[139] By this he suggests that Gloucester's adultery many years ago caused, eventually, his blinding many years later. It must be noted, however, that these two readings, which together can be called "figural", – the blinding being a figure for some error, whether that error is Gloucester's improper evaluation of his children or the effect of his adultery – are two readings that are actually both available

134 Servant. *The History of King Lear*, id. 3.7. scene 14. p. 676.

135 Cornwall. *The History of King Lear*, id. 3.7. scene 14. p. 676.

136 Regan. *The History of King Lear*, id. 3.7. scene 14. p. 676.

137 Cornwall. *The History of King Lear*, id. 3.7. scene 14. p. 678.

138 Wilson, Jeffrey R.: *The Earl of Gloucester's Blinding, Essay, Harvard University. At https://wilson.fas.harvard.edu/stigma-in-shakespeare/earl-of-gloucester%E2%80%99s-blinding* 2021.04.04.

139 Edgar. *The History of King Lear.* Id.5. 3.724.l: 167-168.

in Shakespeare's source for the subplot in King Lear, the chapter on the Paphlagonian King in Philip Sidney's *Arcadia*. Sidney, as a stigmatizer, heedlessly uses blindness as a convenient symbol without any care for the actual experience of the blind. And it is possible to see Shakespeare after Sidney as a stigmatizer as well: surely it was the opportunity to use the story of the blinding as a gloss on King Lear's misjudgment of his own children that inspired Shakespeare to incorporate the material from Sidney into his play in the first place. Yet Shakespeare stands apart from Sidney in the emphasis he throws upon the material, physical, creatural experience of Gloucester's blindness, beginning with the "vile jelly" that Cornwall digs out, continuing with the flax and egg mixture that Gloucester's servant uses to treat his wounds, extending to Gloucester's beleaguered walk to Dover, for which he must depend upon a guide, his son, whom he cannot even recognize, and eventually ending with Gloucester's attempted suicide, heart attack, and death. In the case of Gloucester, Shakespeare is not a stigmatizer as much as he is a dramatist of disability and stigma. That is, Shakespeare dramatized the human experience of blindness as well as the social backgrounds of its meanings. If Sidney was a "figuralist" on this front, Shakespeare was a "realist," but it must be remembered that, in Shakespeare, the figural is a part of the real. In other words, the figural meanings made of a physical abnormality such as blindness may not be real, but the making of those meanings by oneself and others is real, which is the reason that it is best to peak of Shakespeare as a "figural realist" on the issue of stigma.

Julian Girdham's approach to the blinding scene is: It is "particularly memorable in this play because the metaphor 'seeing/blindness' is so embedded in its meaning. We don't have to see the words 'blindness' or 'seeing' in an essay title to write about these ideas: this is also to do with foolishness, with learning, with development, with justice and prominence." [140]

Shakespeare hammers home references to vision and its loss throughout the opening scenes of King Lear: When Lear expels Cordelia, he orders her 'out of his sight'; when Kent tries to offer the King wise advice he says: 'See better, Lear", he is indignant that Lear cannot see what is staring him in the face, i.e. Cordelia's truthfulness and Goneril and Regan's falsehood.

Apart from blinding, metaphoric blindness is present throughout the play. Lear's 'blindness', or lack of understanding/judgement is clear from the start. Fundamentally, he does not discern how ill-judged is his staging of the public love-test as a basis on which the division of his kingdom will occur.

---

140 Julian Girdham: *King Lear: blindness and seeing, Essay.* at ≤https://download-pdfs.com/v6/preview/?pid=6&offer_id=431&ref_id=9084ebaf50dfbceb05ec959691581175_0071bc8f_c28f910b&sub1=0071bc8f&keyword=king%20lear%20blindness≥ 2014.04.05.

Meanwhile, Gloucester is so blind to the truth that he immediately believes the lies of a son who "hath been out nine years" (Act 1, Scene1, 32) against one whose honesty and loyalty he has witnessed every day. 'Credulous' is how Edmund describes the father who instantly falls into his treacherous trap.

Heilman [141] in his essay about the unity of King Lear explains that Gloucester's physical blindness symbolises the metaphorical blindness that grips both Gloucester and the play's other father figure, Lear. The parallels between the two men are clear: both have loyal children and disloyal children, both are blind to the truth, and both end up banishing the loyal children and making the wicked one(s) their heir(s). Only when Gloucester has lost the use of his eyes and Lear has gone mad does each realise his tremendous error. It is appropriate that the play brings them together near Dover in Act 4 to commiserate about what their blindness to the truth about their children has cost them.

Lear undertakes to reason about certain phenomena and by reasoning faultily he inaugurates a series of tragic consequences. His very first error is typically rationalistic: the introduction of a measurable standard, when it is not applicable. He insists upon that love can be measured, as if it were a material quantum of a certain size and shape. In his intellectual confusion he forgets that deeds rather than words are the symbols of love. This confusion might be described quite literally as a failure of imagination: love must be apprehended by images, and the images are richly available to him – not in flowers of speech and verbal formulae – but in the lives of his daughters whom he has observed from infancy.

His failure here is analogous to the failure to understand that a king cannot be a king without a crown and cannot maintain his perquisites by a kind of oral recipe or contract that is a purely rationalized formulation of status which involves responsibilities as well as rights. From his endeavour to bound a value by irrelevant standards of measurement, Lear goes on to still another error: his misinterpretation of those verbal measurements of love which his demands have brought forth, he is wholly taken in by the meaningless abstractions and hyperboles of Goneril and Regan and – in other striking failure of imagination – completely misses the importance of Cordelia's precise metaphor:

"I love you Majesty
According to my bond; no more nor less." (Act 1, Scene 1.)

---

141 Heilman, Robert B.: *"The Unity of 'King Lear"* The Sewanee Review, vol. 56, no. 1, 1948, pp. 58–68. JSTOR, www.jstor.org/stable/27537810.

Thus, Lear invites tragedy by three errors of understanding – errors with regard to the nature of kingship, the nature of love, and the value of certain statements about love. They are the mistakes of a man in action, of a man whose action is a public action, and thus, it has consequences that affect the public as well.

Gloucester, on the other hand, rather accepts than imposes: his trouble is inaugurated by Edmund's voluntary undertaking, without being offered such an opening as Lear gives to Goneril and Regan. Like Lear, Gloucester might have consulted his non-rational, experimental awareness of his child's quality. Yet Gloucester is the object of manipulation; his error is that he too easily falls under influence exerted upon him.

We have other evidence, however, of the nature of his flaw: Edmund's illegitimacy. We are never allowed to forget, and near the end Edgar specifically connects Gloucester's suffering with his adultery, as we cited above.

Gloucester is a character leaning toward "adjustment". He is the only astronomer in the play – it is easier to explain things with the help of the stars. It is Gloucester's flaw never wholly to understand what is implied in the situations in which he finds himself, even if he feels worldly wise enough. Not that he voluntarily seeks what is evil: it is simply that he too easily yields to that in which he should see evil.

While Lear, without questioning his own rightness, imposes his will upon others; Gloucester accepts the will of others without effectually questioning their rightness. Thus, Lear and Gloucester are, in terms of structure, not duplicates, but complements: this is one key to the unity of King Lear– as explained by Heilman.

Jay Halio[142] raises the question what scholars have not very often asked: What is the motivation behind the blinding of Gloucester at the end of Act 3 in King Lear? This question was most probably not asked frequently because the cruelty of Regan's and Cornwall's deed speaks for itself. However, it was not by chance that Shakespeare chose to adapt the story of the Paphlagonian king from Sydney's Arkadia. All signs suggest that Shakespeare had blinding in mind from the outset. Lear's anguished

142 Halio, Jay. *"Gloucester's Blinding."* Shakespeare Quarterly, vol. 43, no. 2, 1992, pp. 221–223. JSTOR, www.jstor.org/stable/2870885.

cry also suggests this preoccupation with blinding: "Old fond eyes, / Beweep this cause again, I will pluck you out" (Act 1, Scene 4, 318-19); and Gloucester motif for sending Lear to Dover was: "Because I would not see thy cruel nails / Pluck out his poor eyes…" (Act 3, Scene 7, 69-70). But in fact, it is Gloucester and not Lear who is blinded, and the justifications for his blinding are more complex than appears on the surface.

Halio refers to Freud's castration complex in connection with the Oedipus legend:

"… the blinding witch Oedipus punishes himself after the discovery of his crime is, by the evidence of dreams, a symbolic substitute for castration." Gloucester's adultery is far from Oedipus's crime, but the connection between blinding and castration highlights the cruel irony of his punishment. Prompted by Goneril's: "Pluck out his eyes (Act 3, Scene 7, 6), but immediately put into action by her sister and Cornwall, Gloucester's blinding in its historical and psychological context has a profound underlying motivation. Though he is called several times 'traitor', but the justifications for Gloucester's blinding are much more complex than being a traitor. Halio Jay sites K. M. Abenheimer, who refers to Norman Holland, who says in *Psychoanalysis and Shakespeare*: "blinding, particularly the tearing out of eyes is the symbol of the destruction of one's manhood, i.e.–castration".

Historically blinding and castration were punishment for sexual crimes. Although mutilation as punishment was carried out in Shakespeare's lifetime (loss of an ear or a nose, for example), there is no evidence for blinding.

So, we cannot feel sympathy for Gloucester. Blinding may have been the right punishment for him but not as a traitor but as an acknowledged adulterer, who is somewhat proud of the fact, as proved by his opening lines. And it is also Edgar himself, who uses the word "precious stones" which was a common slang for "testicles" in Shakespeare time.

This awful gauging depicts physical loss of the eye, and one of the zenith of Shakespeare's play. But the motif of parabolic blindness, the blindness to the truth is a companion of most of the characters throughout the play.

In the opening scene Lear well demonstrates this kind of blindness. He is blind (can't hear, can't feel) the falseness of Goneril's pleading her love to him:

"Sir, I love you more than words can wield the matter;
Dearer than eye-sight, space, and liberty;
Beyond what can be valued, rich or rare;
No less than life, with grace, health, beauty, honour;
As much as child e'er loved, or father found;
A love that makes breath poor, and speech unable;
Beyond all manner of so much I love you. "(Act 1, Scene 1.)

He is also blind to Regan's plotting, to Kent's true qualities, to Cordelia's love and – most of all – to his own foolishness. Also, an outward display shows the need for hundred knights, since they are not needed in the well-stuffed palaces, they are just a show and the proof of incredibly poor judgement of failing to foresee the trouble he is bringing upon himself by insisting upon their presence.

His moral blindness results in obvious folly, when he proclaims:

"Only we shall retain
The name and all th' addition to the king; the sway,
Revenue, execution of the rest,
Beloved sons, be yours;
This coronet part between you. (Act 1, Scene 1.)

Kent urges him: "See better Lear", and the Fool, like Kent, tries to make him see sense, see the truth:

"...nose is in the middle of your face to keep one's eyes of either side's nose, that what a man cannot smell out, he may spy into" (Act 1, Scene 1, 22-23). In the succeeding scenes he continues to be blind, he is unable to accept the reality of his situation. It is no wonder, since he has been an autocratic ruler, never challenged or questioned by his advisors and subjects; there was no need for self-analysis, for improvement of his character. Then, gradually, the weight of evidence begins to turn him. As the critic Anthony Nuttal[143] commented: "Lear must be broken down before he is remade."

This theme – to be blind to the truth – is echoed in the sub-plot in which Gloucester is blind to the nature of their sons, both Edgar and Edmund. Edmund' trickery (the pretence of first hiding a forged paper from his father, then presenting it to him, and by this, convincing him that Edgar is ill-willed).

---

143 Antony Nuttal, *Shakespeare, the Thinker* (New Haven, London: Yale University Press, 2007).

Gloucester seems to believe his eyes without thinking, without considering past experiences he must have had with his sons, and sentences Edgar in harsh words:

> "O villain, villain! His very opinion in the
> letter! Abhorred villain! Unnatural, detested,
> brutish villain — worse than brutish! Go, sirrah,
> seek him; I'll apprehend him — abominable villain!
> (Act 1, Scene 1, 79-82)[144]

The development of both Lear and Gloucester is from blindness towards some form of seeing via suffering. By the gouging scene, and the central storm scenes when Lear begins to see many truths, chaos has taken over their lives and will eventually destroy them. This developmental process, highly ineffectual, is also one undergone by Edgar and Albany, both decent men who eventually become clear-sighted. Again, they're too late. Characters in the play who can see, are peripheral, ineffective or nasty: Kent, the Fool, Edmund.

At the core of the play is a series of scenes which show Lear is changing, remaking himself and, despite his evident semi-madness, becoming more sane. He notices the Fool's misery – he sees and treats him as a human being as he has never done before: "Come on, my boy. How dost, my boy? Art cold?" (Act 3, Scene 3, 74)[145]; he responds to his singing: "True, my good boy" (Act 3, Scene 3, 85) and prompted by the example of the lunatic Poor Tom, he begins to see the reality of life for many of his subjects. In Act 4 he shows a philosophical understanding of the nature of justice and society which completely escaped him when he was King: "there thou mightst behold the great image of authority: a dog's obeyed in office." (Act 4, Scene 6, 72-74)[146]

He himself uses the eye metaphor saying: "Take that of me, my friend, who have the power / To seal the'accuser's lip. Get thee glass eyes, / and like a scurvy politician / Seem to see the things thou dost not." (Act 4, Scene 6, 186-89)[147]

---

144 Folger Shakespeare. *The History of King Lear.*

145 *The History of King Lear.* Folger Shakespeare.

146 Folger Shakespeare. *The History of King Lear.*

147 Folger Shakespeare. *The History of King Lear.*

In this scene the two old blind men of the play, Lear and Gloucester, have an exchange between them: "No eyes in your head, nor no money in your purse? . . . You see how the world goes." And Gloucester answers with the perhaps most significant line of the play: "I see it feelingly." (160-164)[148]

In the same scene, in which Lear's madness brings him to a climax of disillusioned insight, the gnomic Edgar can distil the paradox: "O, matter and impertinency mixed / Reason in madness!" (192-3)[149], Lear weaves Gloucester into his brilliant synthesis of the world and of the play: "...Your eyes are in / a heavy case your purse in a light / yet you see how the world goes." And he continues: "A man may see how the world goes with no eyes" (161-3; 165-6).[150]

Speaking about the senses Judith Dundas[151] states that the paragone of the senses is the step-by-step rejection of these senses to affirm that: "the heart and its affection is the seat of moral life. For Lear above all, but for Gloucester too, the heart has to be educated by loss of the sense and even, in Lear's case, of reason". And the language of the heart is sometimes silence – like the silence of Cordelia at the beginning of the play when her father asks her how much she loves him. Beyond its significance in this particular play, the rivalry of the senses has implications for Shakespeare's own art as a dramatist in which he competes with the painter. This single scene from King Lear not only suggests, but demonstrates a nexus of ideas touching the very heart of Shakespeare's poetry: it is indeed a paradigm for the painting that is, like nature: "dumb".

Great literature can be made from such banalities as the eye/ear debate. To show these senses rejected, Shakespeare must show them in operation, which gives us the poetry which mere silence cannot give. It is not Cordelia's silence, but the account given to it by others, that enlightens us. When she receives word of his father's plight she again finds speech difficult. The significance of silence is also discussed in other plays of Shakespeare, and turns up usually when talking about love and the expression of love. Much is said about it in his Sonnets, for example in No. 23:

"O, learn to read what silent love hath writ:
To hear with eyes belongs to love's fine wit."

---

148 Folger Shakespeare. *The History of King Lear.*

149 Folger Shakespeare. *The History of King Lear.*

150 Folger Shakespeare. *The History of King Lear.*

151 Dundas, Judith. "*To See Feelingly: The Language of the Senses and the Language of the Heart.*" Comparative Drama, vol. 19, no. 1, 1985, pp. 49–57. JSTOR, www.jstor.org/stable/41153155.

As Castiglione[152] puts it in his *Il Cortegiano* (1528): the lover is to make his eyes "faithful messengers in bearing the embassies of his heart, since they often reveal the passion within more effectively than the tongue itself, or letters, or messengers..."

But when we think of lovers, the eye cannot always see the truth... Seeing no longer can be relied upon to reflect the radiance of true beauty, for when the eye is in the mind – as it always is in love – it sees in accordance with the heart, whether or not that mind is on the side of virtue. Such questioning the reliability of the eyes within the Sonnets comes close to the more grandly tragic emphasis on the eyes as instruments of feeling, rather than of knowledge, in King Lear.

Castiglione also says that the highest senses are sight and hearing that are to be the only ones employed in the service of love and beauty. In King Lear the debates devalue the eyes, and in fact all the senses, for the sake of revealing the heart naked. Lear words to the blinded Gloucester: "Look with thine ears" (Act 4, Scene 6, 166)[153]. Here, the literal has overtaken the metaphorical in such a way as to give a better twist to the conventional conceits.

Shakespeare's story differs from that of Arcadia in some respects. In Act 4 two disguises take place in King Lear: Edgar himself and his description of the view from the cliff-top, the one a deception practised on sight, the other a deception on hearing. When Gloucester cannot hear anything Edgar says:

"Why then, your other senses grow imperfect
By your eyes' anguish." (Act 4, Scene 6, 7-8)[154]

But there is nothing wrong with Gloucester's hearing, and he quite rightly detects a change in Edgar's speech as the letter drops the Poor Tom role momentarily. Yet, as if to prove that Gloucester can be made to believe anything, Edgar tells him: You're much deceived; / in nothing am I changed / But in my garments." (Act 4, Scene 6, 12-13), an assertion which of course is literally true, though for Gloucester it is impossible to prove.

Edgard's description of the landscape is not that of a painter, but of a poet. Limitation of sight followed by limitation of hearing: "The murmuring surge / That on th' unnumbered idle peddle cafes, / Cannot be heard so high." (Act 4, Scene 6, 25-27). And when they say farewell to each other:

---

152 Baldassare Castiglione (1478-1529), Italian politician and poet.

153 Folger Shakespeare. *The History of King Lear.*

154 Folger Shakespeare. *The History of King Lear.*

Gloucester: "Bid me farewell, and let me hear thee going.

Edgar, *walking away*:

Now fare you well, good sir.
Gloucester: With all my heart." (38-41)[155]

Here the paragone of the sense yielded to a third: the heart.

But he still has to learn about "the art of knowing and feeling sorrow". Lear helps him on his way by telling him that a man may see how this world goes without eyes, and offers to lend him his, while further he mocks him by telling him to get glass eyes or spectacles.

And finally Shakespeare arrives at silence. When Edgar sees his father, he cannot say more: "I would not take this from the report. / It is, / And my heart breaks at it." (156-7)[156] His heart obviously does not break because he can speak, but his "it is" is very near to silence.

Aronson[157] cites Blakes's[158] dictum: "As a man is, so he sees.", and he adds that

It is also true that 'As a man sees, so he is'. And he argues that a man's sense – perception, his responsive contact with the outside world through his eyes – will determine his "outlook" on the world and its inhabitants, which, in turn, will give rise to forms of behaviours open to moral judgement.

The purpose of his paper is to show how Shakespeare lifted the conflict and the tension out of the realm of merely personal and idiosyncratic. He, as it were, universalized it by emphasising the ever-repeated, legendary, indeed mythical nature of man's distorted vision that leads from spiritual to actual blindness.

"The archetype of evil is not necessarily expressed in terms of 'this' or 'that' character, the alien, the greedy, the ambitious, the voluptuous - not in Iago, not in Lady Macbeth, not in Edmund, and not

155 Folger Shakespeare. *The History of King Lear.*

156 Folger Shakespeare. *The History of King Lear.*

157 Aronson, Alex: *Shakespeare and the Ocular Proof.* Shakespeare Quarterly, vol. 21, no. 4, 1970, pp. 411–429. JSTOR, www.jstor.org/stable/2868426.

158 William Blake (1757-1827), English poet, painter, graphic and printer

even in Caliban - all of them being undoubtedly projections of what the artist apprehended as evil in human nature" - Aronson argues.

The archetypical essence of evil is so often conveyed through the metaphor of blindness itself that the many varieties of evil that man is capable of may be said to be not "as you are" but "as you see" – or rather as you believe you see.

Spiritual blindness is one of Shakespeare's most recurrent themes. The evil that Shakespeare expresses through this metaphor lies in man's belief that what they see is the "true" image of life", even if it is impossible. Accepting the most absurd ocular proof they accept the illusory reality. This is why Gloucester trusts Edmund rather than Edgar and Lear banishes Cordelia. By applying a distorted reality to others, they also misjudge themselves. There is a surrender to the destructive elements residing in a man's unconscious, a return to some primordial darkness, of which darkness, in Shakespeare's plays, is the most adequate symbol. Redemption, if and when it comes in the form of insight, as a rule, arrives late.

"Lear's looking glass is the Fool" - states Aronson. Searching for his identity Lear asks:

"Does any here know me? This is not Lear.
Does Lear walk thus, speak thus? Where are his
eyes?
Either his notion weakens, his discernings
Are lethargied—Ha! Waking? 'Tis not so
Who is it that can tell me who I am?"

Fool: "Lear's shadow. (Act 1, Scene 4, 231-37)[159].

One of the many differences that our senses would bring to light is that between appearance and reality, seeming and being, between what we think, we see and what *is*. And though doubts may arise in our mind as to whether anything ever *is at all* or merely appears to be because we see it in a certain way, Shakespeare's most tragic heroes, Othello, Macbeth and Lear are victims of the same visual deception: they take the shadow for the substance. They stumble when they see.

---

159 Folger Shakespeare. *The History of King Lear.*

To see is to perceive evil. Not to see, is to be at the mercy of evil. The one who sees too well but not wisely, and the one who sees not enough are equally doomed to blindness. Innocence and guilt are similarly punishable before the gods. To commit evil in ignorance of it is no less a crime than to know evil and to do it. Gloucester's crime is ignorance of evil: he committed it in the unawareness of lust. He "saw" well enough where he was going, but did not associate visual lust and all that it implies with moral evil. Edgar, undoubtedly

with his father in mind, paraphrases his father's fundamental "innocence. For Gloucester's lust was not guilt-ridden. He "served the lust of my mistress's heart, and did the act of darkness with her" (Act 3, Scene 4, 92-94)[160]; he "slept in the contriving of lust, and wak'd to do it. (Act 3, Scene 4, 96-97)[161]. The moral evil of adultery is passed over in silence. If Gertrud and Cressida are condemned for their "frailty", Gloucester is unrepentant, and, if anything, proud of his achievements. Anyway, "there was a good sport in his making, and the whoreson must be acknowledged (Act 1, Scene, 23-24).[162] The gods think otherwise, as Edgar declares at the end of the play.

Gloucester's visual lust, however, is only one aspect of his spiritual blindness. By light-heartedly ignoring the meaning of Lear's choice at the beginning of the play and by being blind to the presence of evil, he fails to see what the spectator in the theatre has grasped during the very first conversation between him and Edmund. His distorted vision belongs to the same symbolic pattern as Lear's madness, the eye of the one reflecting the mind of the other, so that Gloucester's actual blindness appears merely as a climax of a process that started before the play began. The ironical implications of Cornwall's exclaiming, when putting out Gloucester's second eye: "Lest it see more, prevent it" (Act 3, Scene 7, 101)[163] are not lost on us. Gloucester's eyes have seen little enough before his blindness. What moral mischief, corruption and evil does Cornwell wish to prevent from the remaining eye? What ocular poof should be kept secret from Gloucester?

Yet his false sense of security based on his faulty eyesight will be replaced by a new and more precious "commodity". Othello and Macbeth only began seeing – if indeed they ever did – with their inner eye after they had "stumbled" into disaster. Gloucester's gift of insight comes to him like the agonising bird-pangs of consciousness itself:

160 Folger Shakespeare. *The History of King Lear.*

161 Folger Shakespeare. *The History of King Lear.*

162 Folger Shakespeare. *The History of King Lear.*

163 Folger Shakespeare. *The History of King Lear.*

"I have not way, and therefore want no eyes;
I stumbled when I saw, for oft 'his seen,
Our means secure us, and our mere defects
Prove our commodities." (Act 4, Scene 19-22)[164]

His ultimate moral realisation of the evil implied in his former innocence comes shortly after. Blindness shows the way from seeing to feeling, that is, from ignorance to knowledge. The pattern that Shakespeare follows is once more the archetypal process from the ocular proof and the evil associated with it, to the moral good resulting from insight. Gloucester seems to echo Oedipus' words:

"What should I do with eyes
Where all is ugliness?"

Yet Gloucester goes a step further when he describes "the superfluous and lust-dieted man", that is himself, as one

"That will not see
Because he doth not feel. (Act 4, Scene 1, 78-79).[165]

164 Folger Shakespeare. *The History of King Lear.*

165 Folger Shakespeare. *The History of King Lear.*

Third Chapter

The absurd interpretation of the Folio Lear

As the last chapter, this will focus on those absurd or marginalised elements that may fit into the frame construed by Jan Kott, yet will not be tossed totally into the abyss of the absurd. Hereby the figure of the king and that of a father will be analysed along all those elements that deconstruct the self in order to reconstruct it on a higher level. As for textual reference the Arden Complete Folio text 2011 will be used.

The first sub-point: The relationship between deconstruction and the absurd on the line of the identity crisis, in which I try to prove that the deconstruction of the character brings to the surface the absurd that connects the classical character as a guideline, the whole identity with the disintegrated identity.

Second sub-point: Identity search, the broken identity.

In this section, to explore Lear's absurd identity, diffuse identity is examined at the plot level and identity diffusion at the text level, while it is demonstrated that Lear's moral blindness is recognized within the process of downsizing and deconstructing deconstruction. I justify his identity crisis by examining the relationship between nature and identity. I used the study "King Lear" or "Endgame" and Marjorie Garber's King Lear chapter from Jan Kott's Contemporary Shakespeare as basic source material.

Third Subsection: The Place of the Absurd on the Throne of Identity, by which I want to confirm the fact that the absurdity of the basic situation, which contradicts domination because it pronounces division rather than unity of the country and unification of the nation, places the absurd on the throne of identity. My primary sources are Jan Kott's Contemporary Shakespeare and Stanley Cawell's Disowning Knowledge in Six Plays of Shakespeare.

Understanding the history of the origin of drama is important so that we can then use twentieth-century interpretations to break down the characters and the plot into elements, showing the absurd components in it. With the words of Martin Esslin, "absurd drama seeks to express a sense of the meaninglessness of the human condition and the inadequacy of a rational approach by openly breaking with rational solutions and discursive thinking." Starting from this definition, metaphysical anxiety, the absurdity of the human state, and the presence of irrationality within drama are the concepts that are analysed. This is aided by an examination of Lear's background, which we obtain by comparing the text of the quarto and the folio.

Based on the introductory study of László Kéry, we can say that the story of the old king and his three daughters is of fairytale origin, probably Celtic.

The time of the events dates back to pre-Roman conquest Britain, the 7th century BC. century we have to imagine. In Geoffrey of Monmouth's Latin chronicle Historia Britonum we find the first version of the legend, the XII. century. He then appears mainly in poetic narratives. It is included in the Gesta Romanorum, and its Renaissance popularity was provided by the Mirror of Magistrates (1586) and The Fairy Queen by Spencer. It also occurs at Holinshead and other XVI. also in the chroniclers of the 19th century, whom Shakespeare liked to use as a source material for his historical dramas. Probably Shakespeare remembered a dramatic remake of an unknown author that took the stage in 1594 and was published in 1605 under the title King Leir.

No version of the story before Shakespeare is tragic. Nowhere does the king go mad, he wanders in the storm, he does not banish his most faithful man, and he does not follow him in disguise. "The Gloster-Edmund-Edgar plot was not part of the legend, it occurs in Sidney's Arcadia with other names and royal characters."

Two versions of King Lear are known: The History of King Leir, published in quarto form in 1608, which contains three hundred lines more than The Tragedy of King Lear, published in folio in 1623. Kiss Zsuzsanna What does Shakespeare write in King Lear? In her study, *The Origin and Theme of the Tragedy*, she explains: a twin edition identifying himself as born in 1608, called Q2, was made in, presumably a more carefully revised version of Q1 by Shakespeare. Finally, in 1623, the first Folio All was printed by Edward Blount. The folio contains a text version that originated later than 1605, showing a difference from the quarto but not the same as Q2. In 1723, Alexander Pope made a version that also relied on a quarto. And from 1765, publishers considered the quarter Lear to be correct.[166] *The True Cronicle Historie of King Leir*, published in 1605, may therefore have been the source material for Shakespeare, which Richard Knowles says matches the Shakespeare text in more than a hundred respects.[167] On its cover is *The True Chronic History of King Leir and his three Daughters Gonorill, Regan and Cordella.* "It hath been diverse and sundry times lately acted," that is, as "they've been played many different times lately." This suggests that a similar piece played by Shakespeare at the time was published, i.e. his work was written before 1605, so the author of Leir could have used Shakespeare's text and not the other way around.[168] According to R. A. Foakes (editor),[169] however, it is more likely that Shakespeare may have used Leir as a source, so his work may have originated after 1605. "In 1608, Nicholas Okes printed the first quartet, which has three hundred lines no longer in the folio, but has a hundred lines in the folio that are missing from Q1.[170]

According to a story known from the chronicles, Q1 Leir depicts Cordella, who survived with the help of the Protecting God. In this version, the bad will receive their worthy punishment and the good will receive their reward, and order will be restored in the kingdom. The names of the characters in the play are similar to those of Shakespeare. Leir-Lear, Gonorill-Goneril, Ragan-Regan, Cordella-Cordelia. The characters also show similarities. The figure of Skallinger and the Messenger merges in the figure of Edmund of Shakespeare, and Perillus becomes identical with Kent. The structure and plot of the drama are weaker, the characters are dominated by a single character, so the characters are schematic: Cordella is angelic, the king is choleric, Skalinger is evil. The storm scene seems to be the wrath of a

166 Kiss Zsuzsanna, *Mit ír Shakespeare a Lear királyban? A tragédia eredete és egyetemes témája.* Tanulmány. Szabadpart. társadalomtudományi művészeti és irodalmi folyóirat. Kiadó: Kodolányi János Főiskola Székesfehérvár. Művészeti rovat 14-15. « http://www.szabad-part.hu/14/14_muv_kiss_zs.html» Available at: 2017.02.02

167 Richard Knowles, „How Shakespeare knew King Leir" in Peter Holland (szerk). *King Lear and its Afterlife.* Shakespeare Survey 55. (Cambridge: CUP, 2002): 12-35.

168 Stanley Wells (ed) „Introduction" in *The History of King Leare* (Oxford Univ.Press, 2000): 9-14.

169 R. A. Foakes, (ed) „General Introduction" in *King Leare.* Arden. (London: 1997, 2002): 90.

170 Sonia Massai, „Working with the Texts: Differential Readings" in Andrew Murphy, *A Concise Companion to Shakespeare and the Text* (Oxford: Blackwell Publishing, 2007): 185-186.

"The first quarto of *King Lear*, for example, which was first printed by Nicholas Okes for Nathaniel Butter in 1608, includes roughly three hundred lines which do not appear in F1, lacks roughly one hundred lines which appear only in F1, and preserves a large number of local variants, which affect speech prefixes, stage directions, and dialogue."

righteous God who protects the good and leads the wicked to the right path. The thunder, for example, protects Leir and Perillus from the killers hired by Gonorill and Ragan. In an opening monologue, Leir outlines the basic situation of being alone with the three girls, while at the same time talking about his relationship with his wife, which is completely omitted from Shakespeare. It gives us an idea of how difficult it is for a man left without a wife to raise his daughters, and how much he misses a boy heir to whom he could leave his empire. Learning the history of the drama, comparing the quarto and the folio, is necessary because it sheds light on Lear's prehistory, the greatness of the golden age, whose disintegration at the beginning of the play induces the absurdity of his actions and explains Cordelia's behavior towards him. In Leir, the two older girls do not die but are forced into exile. In contrast to the optimistic tone of the play, the physical suffering caused by his violence against man, the relationship between the individual and society, which is also an absurd feature, becomes central to Shakespeare's work and upsets the audience by he sees it not as exceptional but as present, and perceives pain as part of the human structure — thus giving the viewer a sense of catharsis. Many differences between the quarto and the folio mean that by the end of the twentieth century they were treated as two separate texts, and the Oxford edition of Complete Works — the shakespeare- i is the fruit of editing texts[171] — accordingly, it already contains two Lear kings: The History of King Lear: Quarto Text and The Tragedy of King Lear: The Folio Text. However, because there is a lot of overlap, the consolidated version has been used for a long time. In 1983, in The Division of the Kingdom: Shakespeare's Two Versions of King Lear, Taylor and Warren published the text of both Q1 and the folio. R.A. Foakes and Arden III. in volume, he merged the text of the quarto and the folio, as Andrew Murphy points out.[172]

According to a story known from the chronicles, Q1 Leir depicts Cordella, who survived with the help of the Protecting God. In this version, the bad will receive their worthy punishment and the good will receive their reward, and order will be restored in the kingdom. The names of the characters in the play are similar to those of Shakespeare. Leir-Lear, Gonorill-Goneril, Ragan-Regan, Cordella-Cordelia. The characters also show similarities. The figure of Skallinger and the Messenger merges in the figure of Edmund of Shakespeare, and Perillus becomes identical with Kent. The structure and plot of the drama are weaker, the characters are dominated by a single character, so the characters are schematic: Cordella is angelic, the king is choleric, Skalinger is evil. The storm scene seems to be the wrath of a righteous God who protects the good and leads the wicked to the right path. The thunder, for example,

171 Gabriel Egan, *Struggle for Shakespeare's Text: Twentieth century Editorial Theory and Practice* (Cambridge: Cambridge University Press, 2010): 167

172 Andrew Murphy, *A Concise Companion to Shakespeare and the Text* (Oxford: Blackwell, 2007): 189.

protects Leir and Perillus from the killers hired by Gonorill and Ragan. In an opening monologue, Leir outlines the basic situation of being alone with the three girls, while at the same time talking about his relationship with his wife, which is completely omitted from Shakespeare. It gives us an idea of how difficult it is for a man left without a wife to raise his daughters, and how much he misses a boy heir to whom he could leave his empire. Learning the history of the drama, comparing the quarto and the folio, is necessary because it sheds light on Lear's prehistory, the greatness of the golden age, whose disintegration at the beginning of the play induces the absurdity of his actions and explains Cordelia's In Leir, the two older girls do not die but are forced into exile. In contrast to the optimistic tone of the play, the physical suffering caused by his violence against man, the relationship between the individual and society, which is also an absurd feature, becomes central to Shakespeare's work and upsets the audience by he sees it not as exceptional but as present, and perceives pain as part of the human structure — thus giving the viewer a sense of catharsis. Many differences between the quarto and the folio mean that by the end of the twentieth century they were treated as two separate texts, and the Oxford edition of Complete Works — the shakespeare- i is the fruit of editing texts — accordingly, it already contains two Lear kings: The History of King Lear: Quarto Text and The Tragedy of King Lear: The Folio Text. However, because there is a lot of overlap, the consolidated version has been used for a long time. In 1983, in The Division of the Kingdom: Shakespeare's Two Versions of King Lear, Taylor and Warren published the text of both Q1 and the folio. R.A. Foakes and Arden III. in volume, he merged the text of the quarto and the folio, as Andrew Murphy points out. R.A. Foakes Jeffrey Kahan writes in The Reshaping of King Lear in his 2008 book King Lear: New Critical Essays:

The myriad and substantial differences between the 1608 Quarto and 1623 folio editions indicate that it is likely that someone, perhaps Shakespeare himself, deliberately reworked the work. In the 3rd series of the Arden edition, which was published in 1997, I will already list facts that prove it all.[173]

Marjorie Garber's "King Lear" in Shakespeare's After All evaluates the tragedy as follows: Yet this extraordinary play, in part a poignant and disaffected family drama, in part the political story of Britain's union and disunion [. . .] That play depicting the dismemberment of ancient Britain by the willful act of the old King Leir should have relevance to the stage of King James's time is far from surprising. Shakespeare's play was written around 1605, and in the period of 1604-1607 James VI and II., King of Scotland and of England, was attempting to persuade Parliament to approve of the union of

173 R.A. Foakes, „The Reshaping of King Lear" in Jeffrey Kahan, *King Lear: New Critical Essays* (New York: Routladge, 2008). www.jaystore.org «https: //www.questia.com/read/126127750/king-lear-new-critical-essays» 2018.02.22

Scotland and England into one nation. It was James who first used the term „Great Britain" to describe the unity of the Celtic and Saxon lands (England, Scotland and Wales).[174]

Perhaps this may have been Shakespeare's first attempt to include in tragedy not only the past but also the future of the English nation. It is an absurd and classic piece, separated on a political and ideological level, in which the old king pays a high price for rediscovering the true values of life.

The relationship between deconstruction and the absurd on the line of identity crisis

In the depiction of King Lear's character, we can discover the presence of a process of deconstruction, which, although a feature of the absurd writers of the twentieth century, already appears in Shakespeare as an innovation in its early modern form. Assuming that Lear's first decision is an absurd act to divide his empire as well as his own identity, we see the figure deconstruct itself at the very beginning of the play. The long process of character construction can take place in an absurd environment, that is, the actual reconstruction can only take place at the cost of bitter experience: Lear must redefine himself and find new meaning in his life, find space for his thoughts and actions.

According to Jacques Derrida, "philosophers have interpreted the logos merely differently when the point is to deconstruct it."

Deconstruction, in contrast to stability, brings the dynamics of things, the constant change, so that life really comes to the fore. Its starting point is a critique of logocentrism, that is, a denial that the speaker exists behind the words as an ontological metaphysical reality. In the words of Derrida:

The "rationality" [. . .] that governs such expanded and radicalised writing no longer comes from some kind of logos, and proclaims the destruction — not the destruction, but the stratification, but construction — of all meanings whose source is the logos. found in its source.[175]

According to Derrida, words and concepts are merely signs that symbolise things. Our statements are defined by the structure of language and linguistic concepts, as thinking is language-based. The most influential intellectual trend of the linguistic turn is structuralism, according to which the tone form of a linguistic sign is arbitrary and regulated by linguistic value, which means that there are internal common forms that ensure the connection between the signs used and reality. The sign thus unites the

174 Marjorie Garber, „King Lear." *Shakespeare After All* id: 649.

175 Jacques Derrida, *Grammatológia* (Budapest: ÉLETÜNK. magyar műhely, 1991): 31. Transl. Molnár Miklós.

marker and the candidate. He chooses a concept from the concepts and a sound image from the sounds, thus creating a system that connects the two worlds based on contingency. The transcendental marker, which is not part of the structure, defines the chain of the structure. There can be multiple markers, but the first marker allows the connection of markers and candidates with the presence of the logo. A biblical example of logocentric thinking is the statement "In the beginning was the Word". Because, according to Derrida, metaphysical systems are based on hierarchical pairs of concepts in the spirit of under- and over-destiny, they are ideologically motivated, and thus lack objectivity.

The purpose of the deconstruction is to break down and reinterpret the relationship between these pairs of concepts. Thus, deconstruction can be seen as a kind of critique of structuralism, which, in contrast to stability, brings to the surface the dynamics of things.

Static structures in the present case, such as the father-child or king and subordinate relationship, are broken by Derrida by means of difference, that is, difference, proving that the meaning intended in writing and the meaning intended by the author may be torn apart.

The parent-child love-based relationship turns into hostility, Leart can no longer be defined as a father, Goneril and Regant as a humble child, just as the king and subordinate relationship is transformed, it will be equivalent, purely human, out of it the commander and executor.

The use of the system causes a constant slippage, thus creating an inherently changing active meaning creation, the essence of which is constant differentiation. A supplement is created, that is, a supplement that can only be described in relation to another thing. The text, which can be deconstructed over and over again, allows new interpretations to be born.

Metaphysical anxiety, which comes to the surface with the deconstruction of the figure and is a feature of absurd dramas, gradually engages Leart: this is how deconstruction and the absurd are connected. The first step in recognizing Lear's own moral blindness in the 4th scene of the first act is the confrontation with Goneril, who despises his national teammates and wants to halve their numbers. This is where the absurdity of his human condition comes to the fore for the first time: as a king, he is no longer the master of his destiny.

Here he learns of pain as a supplement that "hurts more sharply than the serpent's tooth" (1. 4.)[176] It is broken in his paternal nature, but he still trusts that he believed the "cleanliness" he had "laid

176 "How sharper than a serpent's tooth it is / To have a thankless child." (Arden, *id.* 1.4): 642.

down forever" he picks it up again. The encounter with Regan (already shows a shattered Lear asking for and referring to the transferred party country, child duty, and decency. His paternal identity falls to pieces, brings out the darkest side of his new disappointment: cursing his child: "A pestilence on you! / The incurable wounds of the abbots / Let them all emerge."[177](1.4.) There is no trace of the former determined, strong ruler. "The next stage of deconstructing his character brings with it another meaning, a recognition of the absurdity of his action:" I have given you all [. . .] I have made you my master-guardians "[178] No more kings and no normal father-child relationship: Lear's world Recognizing this is defiance of the elements, the projection of his rebellious soul that drives him crazy.This is the metaphysical loneliness that Esslin speaks in his analysis of the absurd playwrights of the twentieth century, here he becomes a physical reality, an absurd character in a raging storm.

The disintegration of a character already weakened at the beginning of the play, "the great structure," initiates the deconstruction process that Shakespeare is already experiencing in shaping the character, contrasting truth and perception, leading to a new, important discovery: recognizing Lear's own moral blindness. With the help of the absurd, he is confronted with the reality of his situation, and once he accepts it, all his nonsense is accompanied by the construction of character that brings with it the acquisition of real identity, thus restoring the classical value of the figure.

There are two components to Lear's identity: royal self-awareness and paternalism. He has power, his will is law and at the same time the head of the family. He appears as a strong ruler, speaking from the position of the gods, likening himself to a dragon: "Don't come in peace with Kent / Between the dragon and his wrath."[179] (1.1.), yet he renounces his rule and divides his country. His injured vanity rises above the king, so Lear ignores the state interest because he comes under the control of his temper. It marks the disintegration of his identity by upsetting the state order and destroying family unity by denying Cordelia. It also destroys the security of society when it rejects arguments and exiles Kent. He punishes Cordelia for the violated vanity. "It would have been better: no / You would not have been born than I would have liked it" [180](1. 1.) The notion of "king and character" devalued by the Gonerills and the loss of confidence in Cordelia push Lear's character into the absurd. It becomes grotesque. The grotesque is a stage representation of the absurd that underscores the futility of existence and the

177 "Blasts and fogs upon / thee / Th'untented wounding of a father's curse / Pierce every sense about thee." (Arden, *id*): 1.4. 643.

178 "I gave you all— (. . .) Made you my guardians, my depositaries" (Arden, *id.*): 2.4. 650. l: 442-444.

179 "Peace, Kent, / Come not between the dragon and his wrath"(Arden, *i.m.*): 1.1: 636, l: 123-124.

180 "better thou / Hadst not been born than not to have pleased me better" (Arden, *i.m*): 1.1: 637 l: 235-236.

vulnerability of man in the same way that tragedy. Both explore the relationship between the absolute and man, only while the defeat of the heroes of tragedy involves the recognition of the absolute, which causes catharsis, the grotesque mocks the absolute in the spirit of experience, but this kind of criticism brings neither excuse nor consolation.[181]

The grotesque always takes place in a tragic world, but here responsibility and failure cannot be passed on to the absolute, which, although strong, does not possess some ultimate truth.

Unlike Leir, where the absolute exists as a just God who ultimately arranges things, in Lear's tragic world, the creator of compulsion replaces the absolute, the Gods, Nature, History, and Necessity, impersonal, hostile mechanisms, but these they are no longer transcendent, traps that he himself has set for himself, sins committed without the guilty intention of the tragic world,

that is, through the division of the empire. Thus, according to Kott, the absolute ceases to exist and is replaced by the absurdity of the human situation. It is in this absurd situation that the great ruler weighs the love of his daughters on the pharmacy scale, making the division of his empire dependent on it. He doesn't notice the hypocrisy of Goneril and Regan, he denies Cordelia, who really loves him. The absurdity of his behaviour, which also proves his identity crisis, creates a diffuse identity. He divides his country, but paradoxically, yet he feels like a king, he wants to rule his environment, "We keep only the royal / Title and his contributions"[182] (1.1.) while becoming a man excluded from society and history. His imaginary identity, the king without a crown, will be desacralized by the fool. He appears naive and foolish, who can only provoke pity in his madness. The deconstruction of his character, on the other hand, creates a new realisation: the absurdity of his action, as evidenced by the disappointment in his daughters, as a result of which he is trapped in insecurity of existence and compulsion to helplessness. "You gave everything to your two daughters / s now you have come to this"[183] (3. 4.) Your speech changes, it becomes degraded, it becomes similar to the characters of the absurd.

The chronology breaks down in him "So, so, so in the morning I will have dinner"[184] (3. 6.) His tone is pessimistic, cynical, there is a sense of loss of meaning. "They say I'm all. Lies I am not

---

181 Jan Kott, *King Lear or Endgame.* Hungarian version: Jan Kott, „A "Lear király" vagy „A játszma vége." *Kortársunk Shakespeare.* (Bp: Gondolat 1970): 152. Transl. Kerényi Grácia

182 "we have divided / In three our kingdom, and 'tis our fast intent / To shake all cares and business from our age, / Conferring them on younger strengths, while we / Unburdened crawl toward death." (Arden, *i.m*): 1.1. 635. l: 36-40.

183 "Didst thou give all to thy daughters? And / art thou come to this?" (Arden, *i.m*): 3.4: 653. l: 48-49.

184 "So, so, so, we'll go to supper i'the morning." (Arden, *im*): 3.6: 655. sor: 82.

fever-free. " [185](4. 6.) "Stay with us. Let's swap places, and not a couple of judges, which thieves?[186] " (4. 6.) The act becomes insignificant because the real conflict takes place on a spiritual plane. Lear's fate will be passivity, which cannot be broken out, as will the absurd characters of the twentieth century.

The deconstruction of his figure brings this absurdity, from which the reconstruction restores the tragic hero and his identity. The key to Gloster's absurd identity is similar to Lear's: the faltering of his belief in true love, which in turn leads him to the closed, immoral, unquestionable violent environment where his eyes are trampled. Shakespeare condenses into this one image the message of the whole drama: the fall and fall of the world. With a single absurd image, he can articulate the horrors of his age, in which all divine, natural, and human laws are violated. The social order, the kingdom and the family are fragmented, there is no longer a dominant, subordinate, normal parent-child relationship, only interest-driven action, self-serving cruelty, deception. The characters become a strong sketch, the air of the scene suffocated, dominated by hopelessness and pessimism.

The disturbing acts will be illustrations of the destruction of feudalism and renaissance values. Gloster, after trapping his eyes, wants to throw himself off the rocks of Dover. He is led by Edgar, who plays the madman. A fool leads a blind man with whom he believes a non-existent mountain. The text provides a multitude of absurd elements. According to Kott, the absurd is also a director's instruction, turning the scene into a pantomime because it is done in a flat scene. Gloster jumps down and then cuts off. According to Kott, "since the chasm and the rock exist and do not exist," the pantomime merely makes suicide an indication, and therefore absurd.

At the same time, Gloster's intent and cut is tragic. He is no longer one of the important men of the kingdom whose loyalty is trampled on, but only a man who has fallen into the deepest layer of misery. The theatrical realisation of this, on the other hand, is grotesque, which is a tool of the absurd. The indelible trauma of his son, Edgar's true identity, reclaimed from a fool, can only be mitigated.

Examining the different stages of Lear's identity change highlights this work out of the four great tragedies and makes it a drama of identity. According to Roy Battenhouse, in the canon of Shakespeare,

185 "they / told me I was everything, 'tis a lie, I am not ague-proof." (Arden,.*im*): 4.6: 661. l: 103-104.

186 "change places and handy-dandy, which is the justice, / which is the thief?" (Arden, *i.m*): 4.6: 662. l: 149-150.

King Lear is unique primarily because the positive characters develop in the opposite direction to the plot. While the plot can be drawn as a downward spiral, their character development can be imagined in an upwardly curving, evolving spiral: an example of this is the figure of Lear and Gloucester; both become better people towards the end of their lives.

In King Lear, the search for the identity of the positive characters, the identity crisis, takes the plot to tragedy. In Lear's character representation, the disintegration and revival of his identity within the drama suggests a central force that is realised through symbols. In both the main and secondary act, the identity crisis is the central issue. The activation of the identity crisis appears most strongly in the figure of Lear and Gloucester. Paradoxically, however, real identity can only be achieved through the hell process of action.

The issue of lost identity follows in the discussion of the next subsection, which for Lear is the loss of his country, the loss of his daughters, and the expulsion of Cordelia. The binary opposition to the perceived and the real, the imagined and the conscious, the created and lost identity can be attributed to the Shakespeare character representation. Perceived and real identity dominates primarily in the presentation of negative characters, in terms of Lear and Gloster's perception. Imaginary and conscious identity, in turn, presents Lear and Edgar's self-reflection. Who could recreate the identity but prefer to keep the old one, the Cordelia.

The identity motif also restructures the relationship between the characters in the drama. The drawing of beloved and unloved figures varies as a function of the identity lost and found: the sublimation of positive characters takes place both through the plot and symbolically. This suddenly lost identity sharpens, reverses, and contrasts the relationship between apparent and truly positive characters: for example, as a counterbalance to Lear's loss of identity, he falls off the mask of Goneril and Regan's pseudo-identity, chasing the autumn king into a storm and madness.

Lear's madness is symbolic: it can be interpreted as an emblem of family ties into crisis. Lear's metamorphosis is paradoxically twofold and in the opposite direction: the hybrid pushes him in a negative direction, losing his fortune loses his dignity during the plot, yet at the level of the text the hastily distributed identity is regained; symbolically comes catharsis, purification, "getting from heaven to heaven through the fire of purgatory."

Consequently, the writing technique, which deconstructs the character by itself in the first color of the tragedy, at the same time creates the possibility of defining the protagonist as an absurd hero.

Identity Search: The Broken Identity

The absurd as a phenomenon is tied to human existence, which includes expediency. Expediency, on the other hand, presupposes understanding. The absurd sense of heroes lies in the identification of incomprehensibility with meaninglessness. thus the inability to think is formed, the possibility of a meaningful answer is ruled out and the inability to do so is realised.

Feelings of futility, transformation, alienation and the torment and insensitivity that come from alienation, helplessness in the loss of meaning, the feeling of lack of perspective, the feeling of aimlessness all show the absurd phenomenon in human terms.

If incomprehension is replaced by understanding, recognizing the laws of being, "by recognizing it, we can change." On the other hand, "the unrecognised law" gives a distressing feeling of opportunity, it moves from a vague background, while the recognized one modifies existence before our eyes, "Páskándi[187] confesses. Unrecognised and "unrecognised law" can be a source of absurd behaviour: thus, the absurd is related to identity consciousness. Identity consciousness, i.e., self-identity, appears during deconstruction and construction, a short-lived entity that carries with it the potential for radical change. It is in this spirit that we examine the changes in the identity of King Lear.

My interpretation is that King Lear is a drama of easily wasted feelings and opportunities, an easily lost identity, the origins of which have become the absurd idea of dividing his country among his daughters instead of togetherness, contrary to everything the king's person represents. The absurdity of his behaviour, that he still imagines himself to be king, creates an identity crisis that culminates in a broken, diffuse, and then absurd identity. Lear can only rediscover his true identity by traversing the absurd. Until then, like the absurd heroes, one must experience the futility of human existence, torment, emptiness and spiritual misery, existential fear, helplessness, the dangers of the outside world, expelled from its lifeline. Once confronted with the reality of his situation, the kind of spiritual construction that re-elevates him into a classic figure can begin.

To present all of this, we must first interpret the concept of identity in order to outline Shakespeare's representation of both classical and absurd characters by expanding its segments. Identity, that is, identity consciousness, is the awareness of who I am. Its design in the social science sense is not solitary

187 Páskándi Géza, „Az „abszurd jelenség" és a halál." *Korunk*.1969/2.Kolozsvár:169.

speculation, but a kind of product of the process of socialisation. The question of identity can therefore be approached from a psychological as well as a socio-social perspective.

My interpretation is that King Lear is a drama of easily wasted feelings and opportunities, an easily lost identity, the origins of which have become the absurd idea of dividing his country among his daughters instead of togetherness, contrary to everything the king's person represents. The absurdity of his behaviour, that he still imagines himself to be king, creates an identity crisis that culminates in a broken, diffuse, and then absurd identity. Lear can only rediscover his true identity by traversing the absurd. Until then, like the absurd heroes, one must experience the futility of human existence, torment, emptiness and spiritual misery, existential fear, helplessness, the dangers of the outside world, expelled from its lifeline. Once confronted with the reality of his situation, the kind of spiritual construction that re-elevates him into a classic figure can begin.

To present all of this, we must first interpret the concept of identity in order to outline Shakespeare's representation of both classical and absurd characters by expanding its segments. Identity, that is, identity consciousness, is the awareness of who I am. Its design in the social science sense is not solitary speculation, but a kind of product of the process of socialisation. The question of identity can therefore be approached from a psychological as well as a socio-social perspective.

In Lear's case, from a psychological point of view (the pain of the annihilated father, loneliness in an unloved environment, the betrayal of his daughters), the protagonist, who shatters, suddenly slips back into a diffuse phase of adolescent identity: relinquishes the kingdom and places his country in precarious hands. Kent's words underline the same thing: "Stay if you want to measure the ground all your teen length / once again." (1.4.474.) The change in the traditional family model results in the identity diffusion that drives positive actors toward tragedy at the plot level.

Lear's madness is really nothing more than a search for identity. In the development of his character, we can witness a regressive process in a psychological sense. The search for oneself is a search for oneself: a search for accommodation for the mind, future, heart, and body alike, providing some sort of allegorical interpretation of "forging the nation together." In the relational system of the act of drama, the truth first destroys a stable, or at least seemingly stable, identity to the reader, blasting the main character to then elevate it again and endow it with a real identity by restoring its dignity.

After the division of the empire, however, we see Leart deprived of his rank, who, in search of the old weight of his words, becomes a Dutch, grotesque figure, rather than a tragic hero, in his uncertainty of his own identity. He experiences the betrayal of his daughters as bankruptcy. “In his paternal bankruptcy, he takes over the role of the fool, putting on the rattlesnake that the Fool offers him.”

In her 1935 study, The Fool in King Lear, Enid Welsford[188] dissects how the roles of Fool and Lear fit within the drama. Welsford endowed the Fool with ambiguity, “giving him a dual role: the king, after losing everything (including his sanity), is reclassified as a Fool.” The Fool makes the king fool. Who is the fool?

After the division of the empire, however, we see Leart deprived of his rank, who, in search of the old weight of his words, becomes a Dutch, grotesque figure, rather than a tragic hero, in his uncertainty of his own identity. He experiences the betrayal of his daughters as bankruptcy. “In his paternal bankruptcy, he takes over the role of the fool, putting on the rattlesnake that the Fool offers him.”

In her 1935 study, The Fool in King Lear, Enid Welsford dissects how the roles of Fool and Lear fit within the drama. Welsford endowed the Fool with ambiguity, “giving him a dual role: the king, after losing everything (including his sanity), is reclassified as a Fool.” The Fool makes the king fool. Who is the fool? Is the Fool the living conscience of the king? Or does the king have to play the fool so that in moral blindness there is still someone who honours him as king and by him his empire?

This is a feature that fits into the absurd drama of the twentieth century, as the character seeks his role, as in Pirandello. The Fool also seeks himself, whom he does not love, for he is not a fool, and while he may speak the truth as a Fool, he is no longer as a Fool. Lear’s misfortune and identity crisis are solved by the figure of Fool. He keeps teasing with his sharp mind while hiding his own identity under the rattlesnake. The Fool is the one who warns Leart of the danger of his path to nothing, and tells the truth already in the 4th scene of the first act:

> Fool: Nay, an thou canst not smile as the wind sits, thou’lt
> catch cold shortly. There, take my coxcomb. Why, this
> fellow has banished two on’s daughters and did the
> third a blessing against his will—if thou follow him,
> thou must needs wear my coxcomb. *[to Lear]* How now,

188 Welsford, Enid, „The Fool in King Lear” in *Four Centuries of Shakespearian Criticism*, (ed.) Frank Kermode, (New York: Avon Books, 1965).

nuncle? Would I had two coxcombs and two daughters.
Lear: Why, my boy?
Fool: If I gave them all my living, I'd keep my coxcombs
Myself. There's mine, beg another of thy daughters.
[. . .]
Kent: This is nothing, fool.
Fool: Then 'tis like the breath of an unfee'd lawyer,
you gave me nothing for't. *[to Lear]* Can you make no
use of nothing, nuncle?
Lear: Why no, boy, nothing can be made out of nothing.
Fool: *[to Kent]* Prithee tell him, so much the rent of his
land comes to, he will not believe a fool. (King Lear, Arden, *id*: 641. l: 99-132.)

In the truth-seeking Fool's speech, the rewarded girls become denied and the expelled Cordelia, who "can't smile the way the wind blows," is blessed as if to predict Lear's later psychological attitude toward his children. The two rattlesnakes are a symbol of a foolish decision against his daughters, and the offering of the Fool's own is actually a desacralization of the king, an advance to a Fool. His speech evokes the humour of absurd dramas: "Can you make no use of nothing, nuncle?" (Arden, *id*): 1.4. 641. l: 128-129. Here, "nothing" is the deceptive love of the two older girls, for which Lear practically annihilated himself, for "nothing can be done out of nothing," (Lear, 1.4.) So the income of his country becomes null and void for him. "The income of his country is just as much / going. He doesn't think he's a fool." (Fool, 1.4.)

Because the Fool knows and rests on the fact that his foolishness, that is, entertainment, is his vocation, he is not really a fool, but a teller of truth, until he becomes a Fool who does not recognize the fool himself, as Lear does: Fool:" The sweet and biter fool will presently appear, / The one in motley here, the other found out there." (Arden, *i.m.*): 641. l: 139-140. According to Kott,"the Fool acts against the foundations of social order, or at least exposes them." He is convinced that there is only one madness, to make sense of a feudal world that is absurd and puts everything on top of his head: "Fathers that wear rags / Do make their children blind, / But fathers that bear bags / Shall see their children kind:" (Arden, *im*): 2.4: 647. l: 241-244.

"The Fool is protected by his rattlesnake, as is the artist by his art." Edgar also plays a fool to keep his identity hidden, in fact, he takes on this role as a disguise for his lost identity. Lear's Fool is the king's first absurd act, appears after the division of the empire, and disappears after the storm scene of the third act, as if his role has ended by accompanying the king to insanity after the insane act as his living conscience.

In the Ethics chapter of his book Shakespeare, Germaine Greer summarises Shakespeare's conception of characters.[189] In his view, the characters do not seek their identity, but strive to transcend self-identity and unleash their spirit. Greer asks the question: how can the liberated, the "mere spiritual" rule the characters? It follows that neither Lear nor Edgar testifies to a truly coherent sense of identity: while Edgar is just playing with the identity confusion, Lear is indeed confused.

In Martin Lings 'interpretation," Lear lives a blind life because he doesn't know the character of his two older daughters at all. Symbolic content is of primary importance in Lings 'interpretation.[190] In contrast, rather than the golden-age scientist statesman, the moments of the agg man's reunion with reality and his almost childlike confrontation with him emerge. The threads of the original tale, the love placed on the pharmacy scales for a country torn apart and squared for galaxies, and its king, turn into Greek tragedy as Lear's sense of identity grows:

> Blow winds and crack your cheeks! Rage, blow!
> You cataracts and hurricanoes, spout
> till you have drenched our steeples, drowned the cocks!
> You sulphurous and thought-executing fires,
> vaunt-couriers of oak-cleaving thunderbolts,
> singe my white head! And thou, all-shaking thunder,
> strike flat the thick rotundity o'the world,
> crack nature's moulds, all germens spill at once
> that make ingrateful man! (King Lear, Arden: 651. 3.2. l: 1-9.)

The storm scene acts as an apocalyptic vision. Lear begs for the forces of nature, urging the world to collapse. Starting from Kott, who shares the plot of the drama on Macbeth and Job's stage, I thought I discovered two storms: one out in the uncontrollable nature, the other on the stage of the soul that takes place inside Lear, and the root cause is an awareness that neither of his rulers he no longer has paternal authority.

---

189 Germaine, Greer, *Shakespeare* (Bp: Akadémiai, 1996), transl.: Upor László

190 Martin, Lings, *Shakespeare titka* (Bp: Stella Maris, 1995): 104.

The spiritual arena is already the arena of absurd drama, where metaphysical anxiety will prevail over Lear. By grinding his identity, he embraces the features of absurd characters who are afraid of the outside world, have neither a purpose in life nor meaningful responses to life. A terrifying vision of a world turning from its corners, where both good and evil fail, the magnification of evil that becomes cosmic with the intensification of the storm that prevails in nature reflects the disintegration of order and the liberation of chaos. The huge statue of traditional values is Lear, whose downfall is accompanied by a cosmic storm - his hellish procession cannot therefore be triggered by Greer's intention to transcend self-identity, but rather by Elemér Hankiss's "silly, childish pride that the protagonist can't or doesn't notice."

In order to achieve their goal, Regan and Goneril strive for their father, confident in their identity and position, by destroying them both spiritually and socio-socially. But their pseudo-identity is revealed and the real identity is illuminated: evil evil. In contrast, from the search for the identity of positive characters, we hope and receive reinforcement, the development of Gloucester and Lear. Gloster regains his denied son, Edgar can assume his ragged identity, and Lear faces Cordelia's death as a result of his tyrannical identity, gaining a real but nobler identity. Their character development is the transformation of real identity into perceived, imagined, lost, and found through the absurd and also occurs in an absurd way, on the verge of death, when the reality of their situation is finally made aware of and reconciled with it.

The identity diffusion presented above is also similar to the well-being of the characters of the absurd drama of the twentieth century. Suffice it to recall only the forgetfulness of Didi and Gogo at Beckett, or Ros and Guil's identity crisis and memory disorder at Stoppard: the grinding of identity, the loss of meaning of existence, hopelessness, and loneliness can all be linked to Lear's wandering storm.

Time is a very important factor here: Lear's character weakens over time, decomposes, and no longer has a shadow of itself as he wanders in the storm. The existential earthquake that hits Leart has an impact on the lives of all characters classified as positive. Kent stays by, Cordelia returns to ascend her father back to the throne. Lear and Gloster are misguided, self-seeking, self-isolated characters who, rushing to doom, experiencing the greatest collapse and the deepest loneliness, produce the greatest change in their identity:

> I have no way and therefore want no eyes:
> I stumbled when I saw. Full oft 'tis seen
> our means secure us and our mere defects
> prove our commodities. O dear son Edgar,

the food of thy abused father's wrath,
might I but live to see thee in my touch,
I'd say I had eyes again. (*King Lear*, Arden: 4.1.657. l: 20-26.)

The striking opposition between pathlessness and path finding, the path found and lost, the forest path, and the making of the inner path open new doors to text interpretation. The symbolism of the opposite pair of vision-blindness plays a special role: Gloster's blindness indicates a path to true understanding, as in the main plot as well as in the appendix, the heroes are blinded one after the other, emotionally, morally, and finally physically, and only then do they become enlightened. Physical blindness results in inner vision. "Lear's moral blindness is infinite in the first scene, just as Gloster's physical blindness will be in the course of later. Lear deprives himself not only of his kingdom, Cordelia, and his royal and paternal role, but also of the role of master and patron, as well as of Kent, whom he exiles. "

Shakespeare places the plot in the age of pre-Christian pagan society. His heroes pray to Hecate, Jun, and Jupiter. Already at the beginning of the piece, Gloster speaks of the proliferation of ominous signs predicting the end of the world, as if summing up the tragedy to come: "Are these last-day lunar eclipses not good for us? [. . .] love cools, friendship breaks down, brothers clash in cities, riot, / strife in villages, betrayal in palaces, / and the relationship breaks down between father and son "[191](1. 2.) In his speech, the vision of a world doomed to destruction appears to me. Lear's hasty action, which could be attributed to his age, could only have been one of many. In the words of Goneril: ``The best and soundest of his time hath been but rash." (Arden, *im*): 1.1. 638. sor: 296-297.

The absurdity of his decision triggers the chaos, invalidating everything that has served as the basis of the order so far. Goneril and Regan's takeover, an analogy from the book of Revelation to the reign of the beast: "And his mouth was as the mouth of a lion, and the dragon gave him his power, and his throne, and great power" (Revelation 13: 2). "Lear hell" is the disintegrating world, the series of humiliation and identity crisis, the storm in its soul and nature is purgatory, while paradise is a prison in common with Cordelia. "In King Lear, as in Hamlet, Hell and Purgatory appear in parallel, the discovery and transformation of hidden flaws go hand in hand." Lear and Gloster's portrayals are almost mirror images of each other: they are both detailed, evolving, and their trend to hell in three

191 "these late eclipse in the sun and moon / portend no good to us. [. . .] Love cools, friendship / falls off, brothers divide: in cities, mutinies, in / countries, discord, in palaces, treason, and the / bond cracked 'twixt son and father." (Arden, *im*) 1.2.639. l: 103-109.

different forms shows the same tendency (when it loses power, when it is disappointed in its children, and when it is socially destroyed). Shakespeare deals with a biblical theme from the second act to the fourth, but in this new book of Job there is no Christian Heaven, nor any heaven professed and believed by the humanists.

King Lear is a tragic satire: he mocks all eschatology, the heaven that is promised on earth, and Heaven that is promised after death [. . .] the gods, good nature, and man created in the "image and likeness" of God. In King Lear, both values are broken: the mediaeval as well as the renaissance. "[192] The storm sweeps everything away, leaving only the bare earth on which the King and Gloster continue their journey and search for identity. The discovery of the wickedness of Goneril and Regan in Lear's eyes is like a mirror reflecting the discovery of the darkest possibilities present in his own soul; According to Lings, in a symbolic sense, they are part of Goneril and Regan Lear. The symbol of the ulcer is the result of true inner vision, and at the same time an awareness of the same behaviour with his two older daughters, which was "a disease in his soul and in the blood of depravity:" But yet thou art my flesh, my blood, my daughter,

> or rather a disease that's in my flesh,
> which I must needs call mine. Thou art a broil,
> a plague sore, or embossed carbuncle
> in my corrupted blood. (King Lear, Arden *i.m.* 2.4. 649. l:413-417.)

The weakening of state power takes place in parallel with Lear's identity crisis during the drama. Under the rule of evil forces, the good will be denied and vulnerable. In this chaos, which is itself an allegory of hell, the devils of hell are the "ulcers," that is, the daughters of their elders. The more the storm rages, the deeper Lear descends into the chasm of Hell, the higher he rises symbolically, the more his identity is worth. Lear's rise is gradual, and the price is to see Goneril and Regan's behaviour toward him parallel to the way he behaved with Cordelia.

In Davidson's interpretation[193], Goneril and Regan represent the iconography of evil femininity, which can be traced back to Eve's sin, as evidenced by the Hebrew myth, they embody ambition and desire for power - so with their dual nature they evoke hell:

---

192 Kott, *"A Lear király", avagy „A játszma vége"* im: 169.

193 Davidson, *A bölcsesség és bolondság ikonográfiája a Lear királyban* (Szeged, Jate,1998).

Down from the waist they are
centaurs, though women all above. But to the girdle do
the gods inherit, nóbeneath is all the fiend's: there's hell,
there's darkness, there is the sulphurous pit, burning,
scalding, stench, consumption! (King Lear, Arden *i.m.* 4.6. 661. l: 121-125.)

Implicitly, these lines can be seen as Lear's identity crisis, a projection of his reverse world. The iconography of the topos of the world at the top of his head, wandering in the storm, takes on another dimension in Gloster's words: "Here is the night," Gloster remarks eloquently after the king's daughters deny their father accommodation. The dark knight heralds an all-destroying tragedy, as does Hecate, the fearsome goddess of witches, in Lear's initial speech when she denies Cordelia.

In his study Identity in Shakespearean Drama, James P. Driscoll[194] discusses identity as a regularly emerging motif in Shakespeare's second historical tetralogy. In his interpretation, four forms of identity are possible: the real, which is man himself, the social, which is determined by the perception of the social environment, the consciousness of what we believe we are, and the ideal as we should be. Driscoll thus based Jung's psychoanalysis: using his concepts of persona and shadow, animus and anima, and personal and collective subconscious. In a symbolic interpretation, he sees Jung archetypes in the character of Lear, the figures of Yahweh, Job, Prometheus, and Christ, and thus draws attention to the transforming identity of the protagonist and the various degrees of that transformation.

Another important symbol of the identity crisis is grouped around nature and unnatural concepts. For both Lear and Gloucester, nature is governed by the gods, in which the parent-child relationship is also based on natural love. It evokes Greek golden age thinking, the topos of a loving worldview that is already overturned at the very beginning of the drama, and the topos of chaos will dominate everything. They both make the same mistake: they trust in a false identity, in a false love, they replace the natural with the unnatural.

For Edmund, Regan, and Goneril, there are no moral rules in nature, they use their father to assert their self-interest, contrasting both fathers with the naturally loving child. This is how the natural worldview becomes unnatural.

194 James P Driscoll, *Identity in Shakespearean Drama* (London: Buckwell. Univ. Press, 1983): 202.

The consequence of the process, in contrast to the natural worldview, is the unfolding of another worldview, a world on top of one's head, in which the ascension of Goneril, Regan, and Edmund takes place on a social level, and the loss of power of positive characters. Lear himself says in the sixth scene of the fourth act:

Ha! Goneril with a white beard? They flattered
me like a dog and told me I had the white hairs in my
beard ere the black ones were there. To say 'ay' and 'no' to was no good
divinity. When the rain came to wet me once and the
wind to make me chatter, wwhen the thunder would not
peace at my bidding, there I found 'em, there I smelt
'em out. Go to, they are not men o'their words:
(King Lear, Arden *i.m:* 4.6.661. l: 96-104.)

The relationship between the symbolism of nature and identity prevails strongly at the level of the text. For example, the repetitive, very common use of the words "bond" and "bound" in the repertoire of language tools is striking. The meaning of the word "bond" means "natural bond," denoting the parent-child relationship, whereas "bound" means "bond". In his monologue, Edmund calls nature "to thy law my services are bound". All this in Vörösmarty's translation reads: "Nature, you are my god: I worship / Your Law." (Edmund, 1.2.466) The exact translation would read, "I am bound to your laws".

The meaning of the constraint, the constraint, is in sharp contrast to the original meaning of the bond, which signifies the natural human relationship.

However, the natural, traditional family model, the love-based parent-child relationship, also breaks down in the case of Lear and Gloucester. The natural is replaced by an unnatural way of thinking. An excellent example of this is the monologue of Gloster's son, Edmund, which contrasts with the natural in both content and text.

" Wherefore should I / Stand in the plague of custom, and permit / The curiosity of nations to deprivve me? / For that I am some twelve or fourteen moonshines / Lag of a brother? Why bastard? (. . .) With baseness, bastardy? Base, base? / Who in the lusty stealth of nature take / More composition and fierce quality / Than doth within a dull stale tired bed / Go to the creating of a whole tribe of fops (. . .)/ Well, then, / Legitimate Edgar, I must have your land." (Arden, *im)*: 1.2. 638.

Of the twelve characters, Edmund is the most prominent figure on the wrong side. He can't accept the disadvantages of his illegitimate origin when he knows that his abilities make him equal to his brother: "Why bastard, why freak, if I hit the scale as well." (1.2.466.) The right of the firstborn is questioned by the "lawful, delicate word!" by stating.

Due to the reversal effect of lowland descent, he decides not to shy away from anything in order to gain power: "I grow, I thrive: for the benefit of the bastards" (1.2.467), he says. He feels that the world of unscrupulous villains has come, where he can realise his power ambitions. It must serve the realisation of nature's own interests. His pseudo-identity, structured as positive by Edmund's interests, is a lying identity.

Edgar is therefore a symbolic embodiment of the nature (which is also struggling with an identity crisis) that the world of politics refers to and that is dominated and stifled by political thinking. In Heidegger's sense, this paradigm shift can be linked to the battle of Salamis: the golden age of self-consciousness, which signifies knowledge and nature-centred thinking, will be dominated by a desire for power. Representatives of this new kind of political mindset are Regan, Goneril, and Edmund. The incarnation of the golden age man symbolically returns in the youngest children of Lear and Gloster: in the figure of Cordelia and Edgar. Yet, not only Cordelia, but Edgar's identity of true love is considered weak; by playing his selflessness, his brotherly love, his brother manages to turn his natural love against his father. Nature and the unnatural thus change roles, the strong identity of the evil thus defeats the weak, according to the plot.

Northrop Frye[195] places special emphasis on the interpretation of three words in King Lear's interpretation. The role of Cordelia in the drama is very interesting, and even understandable, when we discuss it in the light of Frye's dissertations. Frye's keywords for this tragedy are "nature," "nothing," "fool," meaning "nature," "nothing," "fool." To these three logically related words he attached his analysis of Shakespeare's pieces. On the other hand, if nature's foolish mode turns out on its own, or in a foolish world, all values and conventional bonds are lake-wide, then the direct consequence is absurd or nothing. Lear is the only one who fools himself into fool mode. Lear is the agg king who wants to get rid of the burden of the kingdom and is happy to do so: "our strong intention is to shake all the troubles and troubles / Shake off our age by surrendering / to younger forces while we ourselves climb the tomb." (1.1.458.) As the possessor of supposed happiness, he tests his daughters out of passion or as the passage

195 Northrop Frye, *On Shakespeare* (New Haven and London: Yale University Press, 1986): 105. „I'd like to look at three of these words in particular: the words „nature", „nothing" and „fool."

of time. While the hopelessness within the walls of absurd drama is evident, the lack of human values is striking, and the ungodly worldview dominates everything where they are just waiting for someone or something in despair and don't know how to spend time, a few hundred years after the birth of the absurd dramatic genre before, Lear "just fools around." He does not want to become absurd, for he is unaware of the chaos he is setting in motion when he measures love, and in his play he does not notice the exploitation of his vanity, which ultimately plunges him into the chaos of the absurd. A storm raging in nature and in the soul peels off the ruler's rampart, and freed from self-pity, pride, and pride by the madness that transforms personality in him. He discovers the injustice of the world, feels remorse, and the old, great ruler speaks again:

Awakened from madness, Lear is already a new man who realises his mistake and apologises to his youngest daughter. The feeling of humiliation and serial vulnerability restores the vision of the soul, its moral judgement, which has been taken away by wealth and splendour. The convicted father and the denied girl are found, the father-girl relationship is restored, so the basic conflict is resolved.

Edgar is therefore a symbolic embodiment of the nature (which is also struggling with an identity crisis) that the world of politics refers to and that is dominated and stifled by political thinking. In Heidegger's sense, this paradigm shift can be linked to the battle of Salamis: the golden age of self-consciousness, which signifies knowledge and nature-centred thinking, will be dominated by a desire for power. Representatives of this new kind of political mindset are Regan, Goneril, and Edmund. The incarnation of the golden age man symbolically returns in the youngest children of Lear and Gloster: in the figure of Cordelia and Edgar. Yet, not only Cordelia, but Edgar's identity of true love is considered weak; by playing his selflessness, his brotherly love, his brother manages to turn his natural love against his father. Nature and the unnatural thus change roles, the strong identity of the evil thus defeats the weak, according to the plot.

Northrop Frye places special emphasis on the interpretation of three words in King Lear's interpretation. The role of Cordelia in the drama is very interesting, and even understandable, when we discuss it in the light of Frye's dissertations. Frye's keywords for this tragedy are "nature," "nothing," "fool," meaning "nature," "nothing," "fool." To these three logically related words he attached his analysis of Shakespeare's pieces. On the other hand, if nature's foolish mode turns out on its own, or in a foolish world, all values and conventional bonds are lake-wide, then the direct consequence is absurd or nothing. Lear is the only one who fools himself into fool mode. Lear is the agg king who wants to get rid of the burden of the kingdom and is happy to do so: "our strong intention is to shake all the troubles and troubles / Shake off our agg age by surrendering / to younger forces while we ourselves climb the tomb." (1.1.458.) As the possessor of supposed happiness, he tests his daughters out of passion or as the passage of time. While the hopelessness within the walls of absurd drama is evident, the lack of human values is striking, and the ungodly worldview dominates everything where they are just waiting for someone or something in despair and don't know how to spend time, a few hundred years after the birth of the absurd dramatic genre before, Lear "just fools around." He does not want to become absurd, for he is unaware of the chaos he is setting in motion when he measures love, and in his play he does not notice the exploitation of his vanity, which ultimately plunges him into the chaos of the absurd. A storm raging in nature and in the soul peels off the ruler's rampart, and freed from self-pity, pride, and pride by the madness that transforms personality in him. He discovers the injustice of the world, feels remorse, and the old, great ruler speaks again:

Oh little
I've had a problem with this so far. Luxury!
Take this medicine: expose yourself,
And thou shalt endure what the sons of affliction endure,
To scatter the excess among them,
And show that there is still truth in heaven. (3.4. 508-509.)

Awakened from madness, Lear is already a new man who realises his mistake and apologises to his youngest daughter. The feeling of humiliation and serial vulnerability restores the vision of the soul, its moral judgement, which has been taken away by wealth and splendour. The convicted father and the denied girl are found, the father-girl relationship is restored, so the basic conflict is resolved.

In William R. Elton's[196] assessment, "Edgar's figure symbolically represents cosmic confusion, the destruction of Renaissance values, and hierarchical identity". His search for identity shows improvement: he becomes something out of nothing, the support of his father. With the restoration of the father-son relationship, the inner circle, the microcosm of drama, the re-twisting of natural bonds symbolically takes place. To the bonds that, at the beginning of the play, in an absurd way, Lear himself tears apart by banishing natural love from his heart, that is, Cordelia. The upset of the order of nature entails the

196 R. William Elton: *„King Lear" and the Gods* (San Marino: The University Press of Kentucky, 1988): 86. „Edgar's confusion of personal identity parallels a Renaissance confusion and deception on the social and cosmic levels, for mistrust of knowledge and self (Montaigne's „Que scais-je?" suggesting also „Que suis-je?") accompanied the Renaissance breakdown of social trust and hierarchical identity."

loss of the ability to see reality, which dissolves in the storm scene. Lear gradually realises that by taking off the crown, he had renounced his ruling authority at the same time, and his daughters had also been deprived of his paternal authority. He also takes off his dragon-likeness with his clothes, there is nothing left but the naked man, who can already feel understanding for his fellow human beings.

Lear, who converses first with his fool and then with the gods, finally turns to man, sees the striped creature, Edgart, and feels sympathy for him. So, paradoxically, he finds meaning in madness, and Gloster learns to see in his blindness. Recognizing the laws of existence and becoming aware that the sin committed brings punishment with it, explodes the absurd, modifies existence and with it the sense of identity. By the end of the play, order is restored, the natural is once again taking its place in the unnatural, and with the re-love-based father-girl relationship, so is the real sense of identity.

His blindness dissolves with the death of Cordelia, who is also like Jesus at the Pieta in reversed gender order.

And my poor fool is hanged. No, no, no life!
Why should a dog, a horse, a rat have life
And thou no breath at all? O thou'lt come no more,
Never, never, never, never.
[to Edgar] Pray you undo this button. Thank you,
sir. O, o, o, o.
Do you see this? Look on her: look, her lips,
Look there, look there! *[He dies]* (*King Lear*, Arden *im:* 5.3.669. l: 304-309.)

Cordelia's death symbolically takes Leart to purification, to restore the father-daughter relationship, the family bond, but he cannot bear to lose it, so he perishes.

However, crossing the threshold of symbols can open up new perspectives.

By losing his eyes, Gloster regains his true (natural) vision, which was taken from him by the betrayal of his (unnatural) son. Gloster thus regains his identity at both the plot and the text level, of which Edgar becomes part, who will have eyes in the future instead of his leader, just as Lear has the love of Kent and later Cordelia.

The place of the absurd on the throne of identity

"The absurd phenomenon functions as an existence in the man who once had a consciousness of expediency, but in the meantime has forgotten or forgotten with it, and now there is no new expediency, and the old has already faded. In this hovering between the old expediency and the new expediency is the existence and presence of the absurd. "[197]

Lear, who was once a great ruler, presumably loses the purpose of his life as a result of loneliness, licking, flattering subordinates, a life full of splendour, and, like the absurd characters of the twentieth century, he develops a fear of the futility of human existence. he wants to compensate with a great play played in front of his court, whose vocation is to present the mighty ruler and his father, much loved by his daughters. For the success of the play, as a gambler, he sets up the unity of his country, thereby committing the inherent sin that takes revenge, the grinding of his own identity. The absurdity of his actions triggers the negative mechanisms that affect not only his own and his environment, but the life of the entire country.

The play begins with a presentation of social order, featuring the most important leaders of the state, King Lear and his brothers-in-law, the princes Alban and Cornwall. Albany is the ancient name for Scotland, while Cornwall is for the South West of England. Together, these brothers-in-law symbolise the Britain that Lear is about to divide. Already the basic situation is the opposite of domination, it is absurd. This is where Lear's actual social isolation, which he himself evokes, begins as a classic figure with a single absurd act: he renounces the crown, so the choice of division becomes the intentional fall, the choice of the absurd.

Lear's already deconstructed figure is already coming to the fore here and this deconstruction is only intensifying from Cordelia's response. "Nothing," which Cordelia found unacceptable, actually takes over.

> . . . what can you say to draw
> A third more opulent than your sisters? Speak.
> Cordelia: Nothing, my lord.
> Lear: Nothing?
> Cordelia: Nothing.

197 Páskándi Géza, „Az „abszurd jelenség" és a halál." Tanulmány. *Korunk folyóirat* 1969/2. Kolozsvár: 168.

Lear: How, nothing will come of nothing. Speak again.
[…]

Lear: How, how, Cordelia? Mend your speech a little,
Lest you may mar your fortunes. (*King Lear,* Arden *im:* 1.1. p. 635. l:85-94.)

Fabiny Tibor in his study *Blinded parents, seeing children. The "Eye" as a Metaphor in Shakespeare's Tragedies*, he associates Cordelia with Hamlet.

Whether this world is, say, Denmark and Britain - "prison" or "rotten", and that it is maintained only by the law of hypocrisy, licking, flattery, that is, sin, is only the feeling, the thinking, the truth. he appears as a loving and morally sensitive being. Such a "internally driven", "spiritual-eyed " young Hamlet, the Danish prince, and Cordelia, the British princess [. . .] They are the celebrants of the "world," the rejectors of roles and expectations, the renunciators of long-established rites. (. . .) These seeing children are fools according to the values of the world, because their wisdom is from elsewhere: from above.[198]

This category also includes Cordelia, who fights against the "false world" as defined in the ophelia madness, the "law of sin," against those who maintain a state wasted for crumbs of love, "wounded" by Lear's decision, "plagued by a difficult time. ". (5. 3. 560.) He further develops the spiritual beauty of Ophelia in the figure of Shakespeare Cordelia, endowing him with an acting force that allows classical values to survive and be rescued from the chaos of an all-encompassing absurd world. Yet this "seeing child" has no "eyes" and "tongue" against his father to understand the parent's action against the child.[199]

I yet beseech your majesty,
If for I want that glib and oily art
To speak and purpose not—since what I well intend,
I'll do't before I speak—that you make known
It is no vicious blot, murder, or foulness,
No unchaste action or dishonoured step,

198 Fabiny Tibor, *„Megvakult" szülők, „látó" gyermekek A „szem"mint metafora Shakespeare tragédiáiban.* 1999. ‹http://epa.oszk.hu/02300/02357/00008/pdf/EPA02357_Credo_05_1999_1-2_054-097.pdf› available at: 2008. 05.05.

199 Péterfy Orsolya Laura, *Cordélia ontológikus küszöbe.* id: 85.

That hath deprived menof your grace and favour,
But even for want of that for which I am richer,
A still soliciting eye and such a tongue
That I am glad I have not—though not to have it
Hath lost me in your liking. („King Lear." *The Arden Complete*, *im*: 1.1.637, l: 225-234.)

His honesty acts almost as a deviance in an environment of hypocrisy and deceit, where the great play takes place, which Lear directs before the subjects of the world, and which aims to show the great king to the father loved by his daughters. Since his language is "not talkative and smooth enough" (1.1.) he cannot flatter and "speak without purpose" (1.1.) as Machiavellian breakers, (Goneril and Regan) who exploit feudal anarchy to achieve their own goal, are outraged. both the king and the court. The king by not caring about the gift from him, the most precious part of the country, indicating that he sees through his father's intentions, with which he cannot agree, while the court, kicking in customary customs that seemingly disrespect the old king and show no obedience to autumn to his father and to power. He clearly sees his father's intent and demands in full awareness of his stable identity, ("Let Your Majesty" -1.1) that Lear make it clear to his suitors that his behavior is not based on immorality, "murder, murder, or ostentation". (1.1.) It is not for this reason that he is destroyed, but "For I have neither insatiable language nor eyes," (1.1.) That is, he cannot and does not want to fall into the trap of hypocrisy. Aware of his straightforwardness, which he proudly accepts: "What I rejoice in, though I cannot bear it / I will fall out of your graces" (1.1.), with this disobedience he takes up the fight against the holy world. His eyes do not see the appearance, the appearance, but the depths of the human soul. He knows that his sisters are merely pretending love, but they are actually evil and hypocritical. „I know what you are, / And like a sister am most loath to call / Your faults as they are named" (*Hamlet* In The Arden Complete, p. 637, l: 271-273.)

He testifies to a high degree of wisdom compared to his age when he foretells, "What the trick hides, time explains, the hypocrite fails later" (1.1. 465.) even if he becomes denied and exiled as a result.

Cordelia's exile is the first sway of Lear's identity, which becomes absurd gradually in scene 1. 4, where he consults with Kent and Fool. The Fool realises the meaninglessness of Learben's actions first, in scene 1.4, but only later in the same scene Goneril and Regan's refusing behaviour also makes Lear aware of the absurdity of his own situation. He who still feels dominant is actually struggling with existential problems. He had two older daughters, whom he trusted, and who poked fun at him. Negative femininity won, chasing her into a storm and madness.

King Lear is really going crazy. He defies the elements as he voices his fatherly pain, tormented by nightmares, he doesn't even recognize Kent. The disintegration of his world takes place on two planes. In the words of Jan Kott, "it's like playing on two separate stages. One is the stage of Macbeth, the stage of the villains, the other the stage of Job, the main stage. In the latter, satirical clown morality is played out about human destiny. [...] Fall is both physical and mental, physical and social.[200] The king's misery must get to the deepest, while everyone around him, figuratively the country as well, becomes miserable. „How now, what art thou?

Kent: A man, sir." (*King Lear,* Arden *im:*1.4. 640. l: 8-9.)

Human decline comes to the fore here. Edgar is miserable too, so he has to play.

„And with presented nakedness outface

The winds and persecutions of the sky." (*King Lear,* Arden. 2.3. 647. l: 185-186.)

Kott draws our attention to the fact that the naked man has no name. Even before morality begins, everyone must become naked. As in the book of Job. "Then Job arose, and rent his clothes, and shook his head, and bowed himself to the ground, and prayed, and said, Naked came I out of my mother's womb, and returned naked." According to Kott, "nothing is what suffers, tries to give meaning or dignity to its suffering, rebels against its suffering, or puts up, and eventually has to die." Like Vladimir and Estragon. Vladimir: We will never think again. Estragon: So what's wrong with us? Vladimir: Not thinking is the worst. Estragon: Of course, of course. However, it already is. Vladimir: How is it anyway? Estragon: That's right, let's ask each other. Vladimir: What did you mean by saying that it is? Estragon: That's bad after all! Vladimir: As you say. Estragon: What if we said we were happy? Vladimir: The awful thing is that we have already thought. (*Waiting for Godot,* II)

Kott first associates the piece waiting for Godot with King Lear, and the parallel seems adequate. It is precisely from the absurdity of Lear's character that in a non-absurd, a classic tragedy characterised by clear composition, calm discipline, sober judgement, and moderation in principle, he thinks of himself without thinking and fools into telling his eyes how much foolishness he has done. By the time he begins to think, he is frightened by the changed power relations, the betrayal of his daughters, his psyche unable to process the pain, and he is on the verge of madness.

In absurd drama, thinking is the end itself: confrontation with reality, and man's vulnerability. Danger and vulnerability are present together, danger can come from anywhere, at any time, from

200 Jan Kott, *Kortársunk Shakespeare* (Budapest: Gondolat, 1970): 177.

anything. Absurd protagonists are under constant threat. King Lear is also just a man and is in danger like anyone else. Like absurd heroes, he loses his faith and is left with only the madness that helps him get out of pain. Both Lear and Gloster's pain further slices their strong identities, placing them psychologically on the throne of absurd identity. Gloster's identity goes through a sadistic identity robbery while his real identity is kicked out with his eyes. In parallel with the absurd pain of Lear's world, in Gloster's house, Cornwall is the one who treats the lord of the house's eyes, individually, to increase his suffering as well.

Why did the eye become one of the central symbols of Shakespeare's play? Stanley Cawell explains this by saying that "the eye is the most precious and sensitive organ in the physique, and the physical attack on it is the most dramatic of the infinity of human cruelty."

Cruelty, which also threatens absurd heroes, always attacks from the outside world. From here, Cornwall, Regan, Goneril and Edmund also arrive and become part of the space, which until now was just Gloster's interior. Although Edmund is sent, don't see where his father's betrayal leads. The coward leaves the scene. But the rest remains. Physical cruelty symbolises the psychic cruelty that pervades the piece. Goneril demands that Gloster's eyes be fired. "Pluck out his eyes!" (Arden, i.m. 3.7.656: l. 5). Then Cornwall does, "Fellows, hold the chair, / Upon these eyes of thine Please set my foot." (Arden i.m. 3.7.656, 1: 66-67). In the second eye kick, Cornwall now only calls his eyes ``vile jelly". (i.m. 3.7.656. l: 82.) In the absurdly heightened world of cruelty, "Gloster's destiny parallels Lear's destiny [...] He must physically endure the pain that Lear psychically."

It's no coincidence that, in search of the initial despair of twentieth-century modern age, the sound of physical and mental pain, Jan Kott says — Samuel Beckett seems to be rewriting King Lear with his plays The Endgame and Waiting for Godot.

Edgar leads the blinded Gloster to the Dover Gorge almost as the blind lead each other in Brueghel's famous image. And that's exactly what The End of the Game is about: Beckett was the first to see this "end of the game" in King Lear, peeling off the whole intricate plot of it, everything that was external, and the essence of the beak repeated. Clov can't sit down, the blind Ham can't stand up, and he's only riding in a wheelchair. Use a catheter to urinate. Nell and Nagg "lost their salt cranes' ' and die in their trash-shaped trash cans. But Mr. Hamm is still reminiscent of a throne in Mr. Wheelchair. (...) The fourth actor was King Lear, who meets the blinded Gloster and, after a long, insane monologue, calls for him to pull off his too-tight boots. It's the same clamping shoe that the first clown pulls down in the opening scene while waiting for Godot.

This is cruel and mocking, both Shakespeare's and today's "onion peeling." Peel the onion to the very inside, until in the end only "nothing" remains; the "nothing" that suffers. This is called a fall.[201]

Kenneth Muir, who revealed Shakespeare's religious reading in King Lear, concludes, "Lear is the story of a man who loses the world but gains a soul in return."[202] However, the regaining of the soul, the retention of the soul, leads through the absurd, the disintegration of the real identity takes place, the transformation into a broken, diffuse and then absurd, and after recognizing and accepting the laws of existence, regaining the original great ruling identity when he can have condolences. he can feel for his vulnerable fellow human beings and can apologise to the repulsed Cordelia. In the upset world order, even the servants of Goneril consider their mistress to be superior to Lear, and instead of the former great king, only her father is respected in her. At the same time, Lear, who believed in the king's pure ideal, the majesty that could not cease with the removal of the crown, must be shocked to have been ridiculed. He, who at the beginning of the drama was still "himself in the Aristotelian sense of Truth, the Distributor when he handed over his kingdom, and the Avenger when he punished Cordelia,"[203] is in the storm a man fooling himself with his torments, an absurd hero who fears what awaits him. The deconstruction of his figure places the absurd on the throne of identity. According to Kott, "Lear, looking at his character, his stage shape, is ridiculous, naive and silly. He can only cause pity when he goes crazy, in no way sympathy or dread, "just as his death does not cause shock, nor does that of absurd characters. The end of King Lear, like the absurd pieces, is silence and death. Everyone perishes, both good and evil, and according to Kott (id, 176) who survives is merely "a wrecked work of nature" (4. 6.) The world is emptied. There will be no more coronation in King Lear, Edgar has no one to invite him to. Gloster's words come true: "This is how the big / world will wear out." (4.6.)

Writing technique with early-absurd elements thus makes the reader aware that the future, the concept of the kingdom, the repeated word "nothing" have become Lear's reality, and at the same time the tragedy occurs and is fulfilled by the absurd elements.

201 Kott, *id*: 182.

202 Kenneth Muir qtd in Kiernan Ryan, *id*: 96.

203 Kiernan Ryan, *id:* 96.

Conclusion

Starting with Andrew Murphy, many have written books on the process of editing the two versions of *King Lear*, pondering the editing techniques as to which is the original work. I fell into this trap myself when I started this work because I thought the Q1 should be the original since it is older dated and more complete text than the Folio. However, according to the current state of science, there is a chance that both versions were made by the author himself and the transcript is the work of Shakespeare, so presumably he himself considered the Folio to be more suitable, shorter and more dramatic for stage adaptation. The present dissertation was written to resolve this issue, but I do not have enough information to dare to state clearly in this case that one or the other version is more authentic. Thus, I would rather share my personal thoughts, which report on the results of my research work.

The first chapter of this work seeks to discuss the marked differences that can be found between quarto and folio, extending this to both grammatical and stylistic elements, drawing parallels between the two and illustrating with examples. The textology of the two text versions is very interesting, which we will also cover to the extent of one page. The plot analysis, although I indicate at the beginning of the chapter, was moved to the third chapter, because there I present a broader form of the history of the drama, and I considered it important to expand the plot among the elements that can be defined as absurd.

So, the introduction remained the introduction, highlighting the connections and differences between the two versions.

In the second part, we thought that by discussing symbolism, by searching for metaphors, we might be able to get closer to Shakespeare's intention, if it is true that he made both versions himself, and perhaps we also understand the purpose of writing these two works. From a long line of symbols, we snatched a couple and analysed the main characters as well.

In the third and final part, the drama technique is separated from the Shakespearean art in the creation of the structure of the characters, and the author's greatness is also analysed to prove the hypothesis that Shakespeare invented the absurd, mixing early modern absurd elements into his dramas. Lear's character is the central element. We discuss how it falls into the absurd chasm, how the deconstruction process works within the character, the final stage of which is the construction and a new character.

Dunkan Salkeld formulated the following:

An implication arising from it is that no revision of King Lear took place after 1608, save for a few corrections made in Q2. Part of the Lear problem, it seems, has resided in the way the relation between Q and F has been understood. Almost all studies have assumed that F, printed in 1623, must to some extent derive from Q, printed in 1608. On this view, F contains improvements or corrections made after Q. But, for reasons that will become clear, the reverse appears to have been the case. The great majority of verbal alterations (aside from significant excisions in F) happened to Q, not to F. Furthermore, there is no sign that these alterations were made as part of a deliberate strategy of re-shaping the play. The argument here is that, while F was printed later than Q, the manuscript on which it was based (or one similar) was available to the printers of Q. In short, a manuscript very much like F, but without its cuts, lies behind Q. In line with several studies before it, this article argues further that Q is a reported text, but a report of a very specific kind.[204]

This also implies that text analysis and the enormous editorial work these two texts were subdued are such fields that are not yet exploited and need further investigation.

---

204 DUNCAN SALKELD, Q/F: *The Texts of King Lear* ://watermark.silverchair.com/3.pdf?token=AQECAHi208BE49Ooan9kkhW_Ercy7Dm3ZL_ 2021. 04.22.

Summary

When writing a book, one shall prioritise: it is inevitable to take the reader's point above his views. If the message of the book is not explicit, he fails in communication. However, this topic is so complicated, so many papers have been published about it that I feel I need to clarify my point here at least.

First, I encountered *King Lear* in Klausenburg in Transylvania in the early 90's right after the communist regime. I was too young to understand the subtle meaning of it, the critical remarks in the Fool's speech, however I knew I will spend some time with the text of it later on. When I wrote my first dissertation (not yet translated into English) I gained controversial criticism, that time trying to rewrite Jan Kott, but introducing new formulas in character analysis, like deconstruction, the self and pre-heideggerian Lear. The title of that paper was *Absurd Shakespeare: The Metamorphoses of Depicting Characters- the four great tragedy." As* for the current topic, my decision was simple: to present the less impressive, though still considerable surroundings of the text in such a way that may catch those attention, who have merely dealt with Shakespeare in their lifetime. At the same time, I tried to restrict myself to a more scientific subject than before. This being my fifth book, I hope that I could present text analysis in a clear and effective way.

The present work includes three chapters all of which intend to analyse Shakespeare Q1 and Folio version of King Lear. Q2 is not selected for the disquisition as it mainly derived from Q1 and only few corrections had been implied that makes the question of textology more complicated but the present work is not referring to the textual history it shares mainly concerns and analysis of the most commonly referred quarto and folio versions.

1. The first chapter, which generally includes merely the introduction part, is a broader chapter discussing the main features that have been altered when rewriting folio. Examples were also

listed to support the claims made, textual references and also some scientific references have been used.

The main goals of the disquisition are also added to the first part of it.

2. The second chapter, entitled *Symbols, concepts, metaphors in Q1 and F Lear* selects major symbols to show the author's application of sub-themes and motives in the drama. Starting with the character and symbolic meaning of the Fool, followed by Lear, Cordelia, Kent, minutely examining the symbol of centaurs, blindness, homelessness and nakedness, to mention last but not least the other metaphors too, while the disquisition tries to give an ample picture of the drama, uplifting analysis to the contemporary literary theory, which will be used in the third chapter.
3. In the [# 3.] *King Lear –in the first "identity drama"* chapter, I examine Lear's character from the point of view of identity, during which I support my hypothesis about the necessity of absurd elements in the structure of the figure. The hypotheses were being proven in three subsections.

The first sub-point *The relationship between deconstruction and the absurd on the line of the identity crisis* which explores the perceived, real, imagined and conscious, created and lost identity from the perspective of the absurd, showing the existence of the early-modern deconstruction I consider.

The second subsection is *Identity Search, the broken identity,* where the exploration of absurd elements takes place by examining diffuse identity at the level of the plot and identity diffusion at the text level. I prove that the emergence of Lear's moral blindness, within the process of demolition-building suggesting deconstruction, can be explained by the emergence of an identity crisis. I justify this identity crisis by changing the relationship between nature and identity.

Subsection 3 *The place of the absurd on the throne of identity,* in which I outline the absurdity of the basic situation, which contradicts domination because it focuses on division rather than cohesion, entails a degree of absurdity between society and the individual (court and protagonist) that he places the absurd on the throne of identity.

Bibliography

1. Adams, Joseph Quincy. *The Quarto of "King Lear" and Shorthand.* Source: Modern Philology, Nov., 1933, Vol. 31, No. 2 (Nov., 1933), pp. 135-163 Published by: The University of Chicago Press.
2. Archer, Jayne Elisabeth. Marggraf Turley, Richard and Thomas, Howard. *The Autumn King: Remembering the Land in "King Lear"* Shakespeare Quarterly, Winter 2012, Vol. 63, No. 4 (Winter 2012), pp. 518-543 Published by: Oxford University Press Stable URL: https://www.jstor.org/stable/41819767
3. Aronson, Alex. *Shakespeare and the Ocular Proof.* Shakespeare Quarterly, vol. 21, no. 4, 1970, pp. 411–429. JSTOR, www.jstor.org/stable/2868426.
4. Bache, William B. *LEAR AS OLD MAN—FATHER—KING* in CLA Journal, September,1975, Vol. 19, No. 1 (September,1975), pp. 1-9 Published by: College Language Association Stable URL: https://www.jstor.org/stable/44325582 p. 2.
5. Best, Michael. *Textual Introduction, The two versions of King Lear. ≤https://internetshakespeare.uvic.ca/doc/Lr_TextIntro/section/The+two+versions+of+King+Lear/index.html≥ 04.02.2021.*
6. Bloom, Harold. *King Lear* in The Invention of the Human. New York: Riverhead Books, 1998.
7. Boehrer, Bruce. *Shakespeare Among the Animals. Nature and Society in the Drama of Early Modern England.* New York, Palgrave/St. Martins Press, 2002.
8. Brayton, Dan. *Angling in the Lake of Darkness: Possession, Dispossession, and the Politics of Discovery in "King Lear"* Source: ELH, Summer, 2003, Vol. 70, No. 2 (Summer, 2003), pp. 399-426 Published by: The Johns Hopkins University Press Stable URL: https://www.jstor.org/stable/30029882
9. Brooks, Douglas A. *"King Lear" (1608) and the Typography of Literary Ambition Author(s).* Source: Renaissance Drama, 1999-2001, New Series, Vol. 30, Institutions of the Text (1999-2001),
10. Cooley, Ronald W. *Kent and Primogeniture in "King Lear"* in Studies in English Literature, 1500-1900, Spring, 2008, Vol. 48, No. 2, Tudor and Stuart Drama (Spring, 2008), pp. 327-348 Published by: Rice University Stable URL: https://www.jstor.org/stable/40071337 pp. 327-328.

11. Davidson. *A bölcsesség és bolondság ikonográfiája a Lear királyban* (Szeged, Jate,1998).
12. Delany, Paul. *King Lear and the Decline of Feudalism* in PMLA, May, 1977, Vol. 92, No. 3 (May, 1977), pp. 429-440 Published by: Modern Language Association Stable URL: https://www.jstor.org/stable/461706
13. De Witt T. Starnes and Ernest William Talbert: *Classical Myth and Legend in Renaissance Dictionaries* (University of North Carolina Press, 1955).
14. Draper,.John W. *The Old Age of King Lear* in The Journal of English and Germanic Philology, Oct., 1940, Vol. 39, No. 4 (Oct., 1940), pp. 527-540 Published by: University of Illinois Press Stable URL: https://www.jstor.org/stable/27704688. p.527.
15. Derrida, Jacques. *Grammatológia* (Budapest: ÉLETÜNK. magyar műhely, 1991): 31. Transl. Molnár Miklós.
16. Driscoll, James P.*Identity in Shakespearean Drama* (London: Buckwell. Univ. Press, 1983).
17. Dundas, Judith. "*To See Feelingly: The Language of the Senses and the Language of the Heart.*" Comparative Drama, vol. 19, no. 1, 1985, pp. 49–57. JSTOR, www.jstor.org/stable/41153155.
18. Egan, Gabriel.*Struggle for Shakespeare's Text: Twentieth century Editorial Theory and Practice* (Cambridge: Cambridge University Press, 2010): 167
19. Elton, R. William: *„King Lear" and the Gods* (San Marino: The University Press of Kentucky, 1988
20. Elden, Stuart., *The Geopolitics of King Lear: Territory, Land, Earth.* ≤ file:///C:/Users/orsolypl/Downloads/Elden2013-The Geopolitics of King Lear. *Encyclopedia Révay* (Budapest, 1911).
21. Enid Welsford: *The Fool, his Social and Literary History,* 1938, Farrah and Rinehart Incorporated, On Murray Hill, New York.
22. Fish, Stanley qtd in Michael Taylor, Shakespeare Criticism in the Twentieth Century. Oxford: Oxford University Press, 2001.
23. Frye, Northrop.On Shakespeare, New Haven and London: Yale University Press, 1986, 105–106.
24. Foakes, R. A.. (ed) „General Introduction" in *King Leare.* Arden. (London: 1997, 2002): 90.
25. Foakes, R.A., „The Reshaping of King Lear" in Jeffrey Kahan, *King Lear: New Critical Essays* (New York: Routladge, 2008). www.jaystore.org ‹‹https: //www.questia.com/read/126127750/king-lear-new-critical-essays›› 2018.02.22
26. Fabiny, Tibor. *„Megvakult" szülők, „látó" gyermekek A „szem"mint metafora Shakespeare tragédiáiban.* 1999. ‹http://epa.oszk.hu/02300/02357/00008/pdf/EPA02357_Credo_05_1999_1-2_054-097.pdf› Available at: 2008. 05.05
27. Garber, Marjorie. „King Lear." *Shakespeare After All* id: 649..

28. Girdham, Julian: *King Lear: blindness and seeing, Essay.* at ≤https://download-pdfs.com/v6/preview/?pid=6&offer_id=431&ref_id=9084ebaf50dfbceb05ec959691581175_0071bc8f_c28f910b&sub1=0071bc8f&keyword=king%20lear%20blindness≥ 2014.04.05. *The Golden World of King Lear,* Annual Shakespeare Lecture of the British Academy, XXXII (1946), 26.
29. De Grazia, Margreta. *The Question of the One and the Many: The Globe Shakespeare, The Complete King Lear, and The New Folger Library Shakespeare.* Source: Shakespeare Quarterly, Summer, 1995, Vol. 46, No. 2 (Summer, 1995), pp. 245- 251.
30. Greer, Germaine. *Shakespeare* (Bp: Akadémiai, 1996), transl.: Upor László
31. Halio, Jay. *"Gloucester's Blinding."* Shakespeare Quarterly, vol. 43, no. 2, 1992, pp. 221–223. JSTOR, www.jstor.org/stable/2870885.
32. Heilman, Robert B.: *"The Unity of 'King Lear"* The Sewanee Review, vol. 56, no. 1, 1948, pp. 58–68. JSTOR, www.jstor.org/stable/27537810.
33. Hardison, O. B. *"Myth and History in King Lear."* Shakespeare Quarterly, vol. 26, no. 3, 1975
34. Holahan, Michael.*"Look, Her Lips": Softness of Voice, Construction of Character in King Lear* Source: Shakespeare Quarterly, Winter, 1997, Vol. 48, No. 4 (Winter, 1997), pp. 406-431 Published by: Oxford University Press Stable URL: https://www.jstor.org/stable/2871252. p.407.
35. Hornback, Robert B.*The Fool in Quarto and Folio "King Lear"* Source: English Literary Renaissance, AUTUMN 2004, Vol. 34, No. 3, STUDIES IN SHAKESPEARE (AUTUMN 2004), pp. 306-338 Published by: The University of Chicago Press.
36. Hope, Jonathan.*Shakespeare and language* in Margarata de Grazia, The New Cambridge Companion to Shakespeare (Cambridge: Cambridge Univ. Press, 2001): 83.
37. Jackson, Esther Merle. *King Lear: The Grammar of Tragedy.* Shakespeare Quarterly, Winter, 1966, Vol. 17, No. 1 (Winter, 1966), pp. 25-40 Published by: Oxford University Press.
38. Kott, Jan. *King Lear or Endgame.* Hungarian version: Jan Kott, „A "Lear király" vagy „A játszma vége." *Kortársunk Shakespeare.* (Bp: Gondolat 1970): 152. Transl. Kerényi Grácia
39. Kiss, Zsuzsanna. *Mit ír Shakespeare a Lear királyban? A tragédia eredete és egyetemes témája.* Tanulmány. Szabadpart. társadalomtudományi művészeti és irodalmi folyóirat. Kiadó: Kodolányi János Főiskola Székesfehérvár. Művészeti rovat 14-15. « http://www.szabad-part.hu/14/14_muv_kiss_zs.html» Available at: 2017.02.02
40. Knowles,.Richard „How Shakespeare knew King Leir" in Peter Holland (szerk). *King Lear and its Afterlife.* Shakespeare Survey 55. (Cambridge: CUP, 2002): 12-35.
41. Kállay, Géza. *„Nem puszta szó rendít meg így" (IV. 1, 41) Shakespeare Othellója nyelvfilozófiai megközelítésében.* «dissz.»: 16. Available at: 2013. 10.15.

42. Kronenfeld, Judy. *King Lear and the Naked Truth, Rethinking the Language of Religion and Resistance* (Duke University Press, 1998): 107.
43. Martin, Lings, *Shakespeare titka* (Bp: Stella Maris, 1995): 104.
44. Massai, Sonia. „Working with the Texts: Differential Readings" in Andrew Murphy, *A Concise Companion to Shakespeare and the Text* (Oxford: Blackwell Publishing, 2007): 185-186.
45. Andrew Murphy, *A Concise Companion to Shakespeare and the Text* (Oxford: Blackwell, 2007):
46. Nuttal, Antony. *Shakespeare, the Thinker* (New Haven, London: Yale University Press, 2007).
47. Páskándi, Géza. „Az „abszurd jelenség" és a halál." *Korunk*.1969/2.Kolozsvár:169.
48. Palfrey, Simon.*Poor Tom, Living King Lear.* (Chicago: University of Chicago Press, 2014): 29-30.
49. Péterfy, Orsolya Laura, *Cordélia ontológikus küszöbe.* www.varad.ro: 85.
50. SALKELD, DUNCAN. Q/F: *The Texts of King Lear* ://watermark.silverchair.com/3.pdf?token=AQECAHi208BE49Ooan9kkhW_Ercy7Dm3ZL_ 2021. 04.22.
51. Sears Jayne, *Charity in King* in Lear Shakespeare Quarterly, Spring, 1964, Vol. 15, No. 2 (Spring, 1964), pp. 277-288 Published by: Oxford University Press Stable URL: https://www.jstor.org/stable/2867900
52. Small, S. A. *THE "KING LEAR" QUARTO* in The Shakespeare Association Bulletin, October, 1946, Vol. 21, No. 4 (October, 1946), pp. 177-180 Published by: Oxford University Press Stable URL: https://www.jstor.org/stable/23675233
53. Taylor, Michael Shakespeare Criticism in the Twentieth Century (Oxford: Oxford University Press, 2001.):
54. Taylor, Edward W. *King Lear and Negation* in English Literary Renaissance, Vol. 20, No. 1 (WINTER 1990), pp. 17-39 Published by: The University of Chicago Press Stable URL: https://www.jstor.org/stable/43447291 Accessed: 27-04-2021 10:00 UTC p. 18-19.
55. Thomas, Sidney. *Shakespeare's Supposed Revision of King Lear* in Shakespeare Quarterly, Winter, 1984, Vol. 35, No. 4 (Winter, 1984), pp. 506-511 Published by: Oxford University Press Stable URL: https://www.jstor.org/stable/2870184
56. Topsell, Edward *The historie of foure-footed beastes*, London, William Jaggard, 1607, p. 319, lines 18-26.
57. Pikli, Natália. *Hybrid Creatures in Context: Centaurs, Hobby-horses and Sexualised Women* in Hamlet, King Lear, The Two Noble Kinsmen, (Budapest: Actes des congrès de la Société française Shakespeare, 2020).
58. Seiden, Melvin. "*The Fool and Edmund: Kin and Kind.*" Studies in English Literature, *1500-1900*, vol. 19, no. 2
59. *Shakespearean Tragedy and the Elizabethan Compromise* (New York, 1957). pp. 185-186.

60. Stambaugh, Joan.Martin Heidegger: On Time and Being. Introduction, IX.
61. STOROZYNSKY, L. M.*"King Lear" and Chaos "Critical Survey*Vol. 3, No. 2 (1991), pp. 163-169
62. Stroup, Thomas B, *Cordelia and the Fool* in Shakespeare Quarterly, Spring, 1961, Vol. 12, No. 2 (Spring, 1961), pp. 127-132 Published by: Oxford University Press Stable URL: https://www.jstor.org/stable/2867387: p. 127-128.
63. Walker, Alice.*"King Lear": The 1608 Quarto* in The Modern Language Review, Jul., 1952, Vol. 47, No. 3 (Jul., 1952), pp. 376-378 Published by: Modern Humanities Research Association Stable URL: https://www.jstor.org/stable/3719025
64. Whipday, Emma. *Shakespeare's Domestic Tragedies, Violence in Early Modern Home* (Cambridge: Cambridge University Press, 2019).
65. Wilson, Jeffrey R.: *The Earl of Gloucester's Blinding, Essay, Harvard University. At https://wilson.fas.harvard.edu/stigma-in-shakespeare/earl-of-gloucester%E2%80%99s-blinding* 2021.04.04.
66. Wither, George *A Collection of Emblemes, Ancient and Moderne*, London, printed by Augustine Matthews, 1635, sig. A2r.

www.ingramcontent.com/pod-product-compliance
Lightning Source LLC
Chambersburg PA
CBHW042104160726
48295CB00017B/983

* 9 7 8 1 9 5 9 2 2 4 2 9 7 *